Changing Our Lives

Changing Our Lives:

Doing Women's Studies

Edited by
Gabriele Griffin

Pluto **Press**

LONDON • BOULDER, COLORADO

First published 1994 by
Pluto Press
345 Archway Road
London N6 5AA
and
5500 Central Avenue
Boulder, Colorado 80301, USA

British Library Cataloguing in Publication Data
A catalogue record for this book is available from
the British Library

Library of Congress Cataloging in Publication Data
Changing our lives: doing women's studies / edited by Gabriele
    Griffin
    192p. 22cm.
    Includes bibliographical references and index.
    ISBN 0-7453-0752-3 (cloth)
    1. Women's studies–Great Britain. I. Griffin, Gabriele.
HQ1180.G7C58 1994
305.4'07–dc20   94-382
                                                              CIP

ISBN 0 7453 0752 3 hardback

Designed and produced for Pluto Press by
Chase Production Services, Chipping Norton, OX7 5QR
Typeset by Stanford DTP Services, Milton Keynes, MK17 9JP
Printed in Finland by WSOY

For the Women in Women's Studies,
textual and actual

Contents

Notes on Contributors

Deborah: A Black woman in her 30s, mother of two and divorced, she took up Women's Studies at undergraduate level after an Access course and years out of education, and thus found out about the Women's Movement in St Vincent, from where – she is now proud to state – she originates.

Peggy: A Canadian woman in her early 40s who came to Britain in the 1970s, did many things as well as being a middle-class housewife and mother, and finally took a degree in Women's Studies, gaining confidence in her (academic) self and producing a dissertation which reviewed the notion that anorectics are young girls who either die or are cured.

Suki: A mixed-race woman with a history of modelling and a course in Business Studies, who was 'talked into' doing Women's Studies modules on an undergraduate degree course and used making a tape-slide on the course to reconsider her relationship with her Trinidadian father. She does not take to sexism, having been on the receiving end of it.

Elspeth: A woman in her 50s with a long-standing history of involvement in women's groups and in teaching Women's Studies without a Women's Studies degree, a long-term feminist and accomplished potter, Elspeth did an MA in Women's Studies in what seems to her a slightly ungracious fashion. Her main joy on the course was learning how to make videos and doing a video about herself and her sister which influenced that relationship tremendously, and for the better.

Chris: Chris's career as a schoolteacher in sciences was cut short by illness; having to rethink her future, she embarked on an MA in Women's Studies to effect a complete break with her past. Her dissertation on inclusive language in the church (arising out of an attempt to work out why she did not feel addressed by what was said during sermons) led straight to a PhD in the same area.

M: An Argentinian woman in her early 40s, M has been in Britain for more than 20 years. Having been a wife and mother and worked in Basic Adult Education for a while, as well as having had some experiences in women's groups, M was hungry for intellectual stimulation and wanted to meet feminist women, in order to propel herself into action. So she joined an MA in Women's Studies.

Sue: A schoolteacher with a general arts background and a desire for group work, Sue joined an MA in Women's Studies. As the only lesbian there, and initially overwhelmed by being in crowded seminars, she was quiet on the course to begin with. She developed an intense interest in making videos and in feminist film theory. This led on to her current PhD work on feminist film-makers.

Ruth: A mother and wife, teaching part-time in her daughter's school, Ruth wanted to get out of the rut she felt she was in and applied to do an MA in Women's Studies. This made her reconsider her past experiences with women, such as being the headmistress' pet and then falling from grace, provided her – eventually – with new female friends, and encouraged her to do work on the lives of her aunt and the aunt's female friend.

Gina: A woman of 60, with an upper-middle-class, quasi-Victorian upbringing, a past of bringing up four children by herself, a history of being Chairwoman of the Education Committee of her local council, an active Tory, and a governor at the college where she decided to attend an MA in Women's Studies, she wanted to encounter the challenge of feminism, to the amazement and delight of her tutors.

Celia Kitzinger teaches Social Psychology and Women's Studies at Loughborough University. She is author of *The Social Construction of Lesbianism* (Sage, 1987), and co-author (with Sue Wilkinson) of *Heterosexuality: A 'Feminism & Psychology' Reader* (Sage, 1993). Her most recent book (co-authored with Rachel Perkins) is *Changing our Minds: Lesbian Feminism & Psychology* (Onlywomen Press, 1993).

Maggie Humm is Co-ordinator of Women's Studies at the University of East London, currently Britain's only full undergraduate degree in Women's Studies. A Visiting Professor of Women's Studies at the Queen's University, Belfast, she is author of *Border Traffic: Strategies of Contemporary Women Writers* (Manchester University Press, 1991) and of *Feminist Criticism: A Dictionary of Feminist Theory* (Harvester Wheatsheaf, 1986). She is editor of *Feminisms: A Reader* (Harvester Wheatsheaf, 1992), *A Reader's Guide to Contemporary Feminist Literary Criticism* (Harvester Wheatsheaf, 1991) and co-editor of *The International Handbook of Women's Studies* (Harvester Wheatsheaf, 1993). Current work includes being subject editor of the *International Encyclopedia of Women's Studies* (Harvester Wheatsheaf) and doing research on *Practising Feminist Criticism* (Harvester Wheatsheaf) and *Feminism and Film* (Polity Press).

Lynne Pearce teaches English and Women's Studies at Lancaster University. She is co-author of *Feminist Readings/Feminists Reading* (Harvester Wheatsheaf, 1989), and author of *Woman/Image/Text* (Harvester Wheatsheaf, 1991) and of *Reading Dialogues* (Edward Arnold, 1994). Her next project, *Feminism and the Politics of Reading*, will combine a selection of her published essays on 'reader positioning' with some new ones, focusing, in particular, on the 'emotional politics' of the reading process. She also has a (strictly textual) interest in romance: *Romance Revisited* (Lawrence and Wishart), edited with Jackie Stacey, will appear in 1994.

Penelope Kenrick teaches Women's Studies and Art History at Anglia Polytechnic University, Cambridge. She has produced educational videos on the artist Susan Hiller. Her research interests focus on contemporary feminist artists such as Mary Kelly and Barbara Krüger.

Joanna de Groot teaches History and Women's Studies at the University of York. Her academic interests fall into three particular areas. Doing work on the history of the Middle East has stimulated her concern with cultural differences, cultural comparison and cultural encounters. Her interest (practical as well as academic) in women's experience of political movements and political activism has nurtured work on the dynamics of gender in society and politics (past and present) in both its material and cultural aspects. Her studies of relations between the 'cultural' and 'material' dimensions of social work for women, and of the articulation of gender within other structures of power, difference and inequality, have generated an interest in questions of theory, method and concepts in Women's Studies. ·

Gabriele Griffin teaches Women's Studies and Modern English Studies at Nene College, Northampton. She is editor of *Difference in View: Women and Modernism* (Falmer, 1994) and of *Outwrite: Lesbianism and Popular Culture* (Pluto, 1993). She co-edited *Stirring It: Challenges for Feminism* (Falmer, 1994), and wrote *Heavenly Love? Lesbian Images in Twentieth-Century Women's Writing* (Manchester University Press, 1993). At the moment she is working on maternal grotesques, and on AIDS and representation, as well as on women's theatre.

Acknowledgements

Gabriele Griffin would like to thank the following for granting her permission to use (excerpts from) their poems/poems for which they hold copyright:

Aspen © for use of an excerpt from her poem 'For My "Apolitical" Sisters', and especially for one line (she knows which) which we discussed a lot on the phone, first published in *One Foot on the Mountain*, ed. Lilian Mohin (London: Onlywomen Press, 1980) and subsequently reprinted in *In the Pink*, eds. The Raving Beauties (London: Women's Press, 1983).
Judith Barrington © for excerpts from 'Where are the brave new worlds' and 'A million marching women', both of which appear in *One Foot on the Mountain*, ed. Lilian Mohin (London: Onlywomen Press, 1980).
Jean Binta Breeze © and Virago Press © for 'Mother ... Sister ... Daughter ...' from *Spring Cleaning* by Jean Binta Breeze (London: Virago, 1992).
Ruth Fainlight © for excerpts from 'Definition' which appeared in *The Bloodaxe Book of Contemporary Women Poets*, ed. Jeni Couzyn (Newcastle upon Tyne: Bloodaxe, 1985).
Fiona Norris © for an excerpt from 'Classroom Politics' which was published in *No Holds Barred*, eds. The Raving Beauties (London: Women's Press, 1985).

'Who Said It Was Simple' by Audre Lorde. Copyright © The Estate of Audre Lorde, 1993. From UNDERSONG, published by Virago Press, 1993. Special thanks to Jo Forshaw of Virago Press for being very helpful with last-minute requests.

The lines from 'Cartographies of Silence,' 'For Memory,' and 'Prospective Immigrants Please Note' are reprinted from THE FACT OF A DOORFRAME, Poems Selected and New, 1950–1984, By Adrienne Rich, by permission of the author and W.W. Norton & Company, Inc. Copyright © 1984 by Adrienne Rich. Copyright © 1975, 1978 by W.W. Norton & Company, Inc. Copyright © 1981 by Adrienne Rich.

Gabriele Griffin would also like to thank Helen Windrath of the Women's Press and Lilian Mohin of Onlywomen Press for offering prompt and constructive support in trying to trace women poets; Aspen and Fiona Norris for getting in touch with lightning speed; Judith Barrington and Ruth Fainlight for granting permissions gracefully and freely; Anne Beech of Pluto Press for being supportive with this project; Maggie Humm and Penelope Kendrick for suggestions and advice; Nene College for granting remission from teaching; and, finally and especially, all the women whose account of doing Women's Studies appear in this volume which was only possible because they were prepared to give time and effort to recounting their experiences.

Introduction

GABRIELE GRIFFIN

This book is about women's experiences in and of Women's Studies. It is for women wanting to get involved in Women's Studies who would like to understand how other women have experienced such courses and how that experience has fitted into their lives. It also provides some ideas of how experience can be used in Women's Studies, how specific practices on courses – such as making videos and tape-slides, or writing autobiographically – can utilise women's personal experiences and transform them. Additionally, this book is for women who are already or have been on Women's Studies courses and who want to take stock of their experiences on such a course, of how they work/ed within it and how that compares to other women's experiences.

The impetus for *Changing Our Lives* came from my experiences of talking with women who want to join the MA in Women's Studies on which I teach and with women who are on Women's Studies courses both in my institution, Nene College in Northampton, and elsewhere. What struck me in talking to these women were three things:

1) They often, though not invariably, did not have a very clear idea of what Women's Studies might be about, other than that in some way it would be about women and that it would possibly (or they hoped it would) be feminist.
2) They felt addressed by the subject in personal, yet sometimes not clearly specifiable ways (many said, 'I want to do/am doing Women's Studies *for myself*'), *and* were sometimes worried about the implications of this ('Will I change out of all recognition if I do this subject?'; 'Do I have to be a feminist/a lesbian to do it?').
3) Many women felt that the pre-course reading lists they had been given had not completely addressed what they wanted to know, and that they would have liked more information about the experience of Women's Studies.

To deal with the first and last points together, the growth of Women's Studies in Britain in the last 15 years has led to much work being done and published in this field, which Women's Studies courses can now draw on. *Half the Sky: An Introduction to Women's Studies* by the Bristol Women's Studies Group, published in 1979, was probably the first Women's Studies anthology in Britain offering a menu for a Women's Studies course with chapters on growing up female, education, bodies and minds, marriage, motherhood, work and creativity. A similar anthology, but less of a how-to book, followed *Half the Sky* in 1982: the Open University's *The Changing Experience of Women*. These texts provide some indication as to what Women's Studies is about in terms of the kinds of topics covered.

In 1979 the editors of *Half the Sky* wrote: 'None of us are full-time teachers of women's studies, but we have all taught courses about women in a variety of contexts, primarily in Adult Education (Bristol Women's Studies' Group 1979, p. 3). Women's Studies was knocking on the doors of academe in Britain but it only gained admittance in the early 1980s. Out of the struggles to gain entry and acceptance within tertiary education grew Gloria Bowles and Renate Duelli Klein's *Theories of Women's Studies* (1983), which addressed questions of Women's Studies as an academic discipline, the place of theory within Women's Studies and issues of feminist methodology.

Since then, issues of content and of methodology have dominated Women's Studies-related texts. Women's Studies is now an established academic discipline, as evidenced by the large number of texts in the area published in the early 1990s. Anthologies such as Diane Richardson and Victoria Robinson's *Introducing Women's Studies* contain essays specifically written for these compilations on a variety of areas commonly taught on Women's Studies courses, for example feminist theory, violence towards women, sexuality, women and health, women and reproduction. There are also collections of excerpts from other important essays and texts, brought together to provide easy access and introduction to a wide range of diverse sources. Maggie Humm's *Feminisms: A Reader* and Stevi Jackson *et al*'s *Women's Studies: A Reader* are good examples of the latter. Additionally, there are many texts on feminist theories and feminist methodologies, some of which I have listed in the References and Further Reading section at the end of this introduction.

All these books form the backbone of many Women's Studies reading lists. But often they do not address the issue of the experience of doing Women's Studies, why women decide to do it and what impact it has on them. The British (as opposed to North

American) texts which have dealt with that experience in the most sustained way are the ones published by Falmer which have arisen out of the annual Women's Studies Network (UK) Association conferences: Jane Aaron and Sylvia Walby's *Out of the Margins: Women's Studies in the Nineties* (1991), Hilary Hinds' *et al*'s *Working Out: New Directions for Women's Studies* (1992), Mary Kennedy *et al*'s *Making Connections: Women's Studies, Women's Movements, Women's Lives* (1993) and Gabriele Griffin *et al*'s *Stirring It: Challenges for Feminism* (1994). Each of these volumes contains several essays which focus on the experience of doing Women's Studies. They do so in the context of *difference and inequality*, meaning as part of a discussion which highlights how diverse groups of women have different experiences in Women's Studies because of the kinds of women they are. Differences among women, the way in which particular groups of women are perceived or treated in Women's Studies because they are lesbian or Black or working-class or disabled, are thus the issue which informs these particular discussions of the experience of doing Women's Studies. Women's inadvertent or deliberate oppression of other women is highlighted.

But other concerns – for instance, what women want, or are expressing when they choose to attend a Women's Studies course, whether or not doing Women's Studies means being or having to be a feminist, how doing Women's Studies will affect women – are not as a matter of course covered in these kinds of essays. Yet they are also important issues. Women coming to Women's Studies do not only want to know about the content of the courses but what effects the courses are likely to have on them. One wants to be prepared, even if 'being prepared' is an illusion.

In some respects it is always the case that one desires to have an experience, whatever it is, before one actually has it. The theory is that if only you know what it is like, then you will be able to act in an appropriate manner when the time comes. Many women's magazines' problem pages, especially those in magazines addressed to younger women, are full of letters expressing the desire to know what something (kissing, sexual intercourse, etc.) might be like so that we will be prepared for it. We often ask, 'What was it like?' to gain insight into an experience we have not (yet) had. Consider the news media homing in on people who have had a 'newsworthy' experience, whether positive or negative. Frequently, these people are asked, 'How did you feel when ...?' We want to know what it was or is like. We hope to learn from others' experiences, to be prepared to say either, 'I shall not be like that,' or, 'Yes, I'm going to do that.'

On one level, it is of course impossible to have an experience without having it as such, to have a virtual experience or to live vicariously – this can never be the same as any actual experience. There is always a gap between fantasy and reality; we may be able to construct a fantasy and be 'in control' of that, but we cannot control the reality of others, whether these are people or other factors (such as the weather, to name a very banal example) who/which are part of an actual experience. So, unless we have the experience, its precise impact will always elude us. Furthermore, other people's experience of an event, or, for that matter, a Women's Studies course, will never be exactly like ours because their history, their expectations, the factors which influence their lives will differ from ours. Other people's experiences can thus only be representative to a limited degree.

Nonetheless, we desire and like others' narratives of their experiences. Witness the avid reading of (auto)biographies, for instance, or the fact that women tend to read the problem page in magazines first. Making comparisons is one basic way in which we regulate our lives, decide what we do and what we do not want. The possibility of comparison offers reassurance. We make sense of our experiences in the light of what other people tell us about theirs.

One source of knowledge about the experience of doing Women's Studies and its impact are other women who are or have been involved in Women's Studies. Due to the fact that Women's Studies is not yet taught at school level, that it has only become established as a discipline in British academe in the last few years, that it often operates without departmental bases and that Women's Studies students are employable in a vast range of areas, not all women will necessarily have met someone who has done Women's Studies. It is for this reason that the central section of this book is devoted to first-person narratives by Women's Studies students.

The nine students whose views are included here represent a sample of Women's Studies students which does not and cannot cover all the different kinds of Women's Studies students there are. But the interviewees range in age from their early 30s to their 60s. They come from diverse class backgrounds. Some were born in Britain, some came to Britain at different stages of their development. The ethnic backgrounds of the women vary tremendously; one woman is Argentinian, one Canadian, one came from St Vincent, another is of mixed race, some are English. Politically, some are liberal, some left-wing, one is a card-carrying Tory. Their educational backgrounds range from little formal education to having previously done at least one degree. Some are single, some are married or live with partners. One interviewee is a lesbian, the others appear to be heterosexual. One woman is disabled. Two of the women attended an undergraduate modular Women's Studies course; the rest were doing an MA in Women's Studies courses in diverse institutions and locations. In this respect, these women parallel Women's Studies courses in Britain in the early 1990s, in that in this subject there are still many more free-standing postgraduate courses than undergraduate ones. The women's reasons for coming to Women's Studies courses varied as much as their actual course experiences did. Not all would have identified themselves as feminists when they started their Women's Studies courses, but by the end of the courses they all did.

I wanted to include as many different women as possible in this volume and the women whose voices are included were selected on the basis of their diversity. I 'found' them by getting in touch with tutors I know on Women's Studies courses and asking them if they had any students whom they thought might be willing to participate. The tutors suggested a number of students and I then got in touch with these, telling them what the project was about and arranging to see them either in their homes (if I did not know the students) or in the institutional setting that they knew. I interviewed one woman whom I had not met before in the London Student Union Building, and one whom I did know at my house. With two exceptions, the interviews thus took place in surroundings with which the women were very familiar.

It is of course difficult to judge what effects the interview situation had on what the women said. Texts such as Liz Stanley and Sue Wise's *Breaking Out Again* and Sherna Berger Gluck and Daphne Patai's *Women's Words* provide extended discussions of feminist concerns around interviewing. In relation to the present project, there were certain clear differences both between the interviewees and myself, and across the interview situations themselves. I knew some of the women reasonably well, others not at all. They had all been or still were Women's Studies students, I am a Women's Studies tutor and I was putting the project together. This difference was to some extent mediated by the fact that the women had agreed to participate, knew what the project was about and for, were told in advance that they would receive copies of the transcripts of their interviews which they could then edit, and that that is what happened. Confidentiality was preserved by identifying the women only by first names or initials, and by not using the names of specific other people or institutions.

I decided on interviewing the Women's Studies students rather than asking them to write a piece about their experiences of doing Women's Studies because I thought they would find it easier to talk about rather than to write up that experience. Writing is quite a daunting and time-consuming thing to do, and asking someone who is very busy and is possibly having to produce coursework for a Women's Studies course to do a sustained piece of writing about their experiences of Women's Studies could be very demanding. I am certain that some of the women, at least, would not have participated in this project if they had had to write rather than talk about their experiences – not because they were unwilling to do so but because of constraints on their time.

As it was, I taped the interviews, then transcribed them, dividing them into subsections, and then sent them to the women for their comments and emendations. I incorporated the women's changes into the interview transcripts and then sent out the revised version for final approval. The final version of each interview as it appears in this volume is the one agreed by the woman who was interviewed.

The women's responses to the transcriptions of their interviews were interesting. All felt in one way or another surprised by what they'd said or how they seemed to 'sound'. Just as one is always taken aback by how one sounds on tape or how one looks on video, so the interviewees were surprised by how they 'sounded'. This was partly due to the fact that they were reading transcriptions of an *oral* exchange, and that this orality manifests itself in the vocabulary they use. For them, as for the readers of this book, it is important to remember that Section II consists of edited transcripts of interviews that were orally conducted.

Second, the interviewees were not only surprised by how they had talked but by what they had said. Most of them felt an initial urge to rewrite their whole text, wanting to make it somehow 'better', more complete, more accurate. Some felt they had not always been clear about the details of their lives and experiences. Some women wanted to rewrite sections where they felt they had been too strong or partial in their views. Most were at least a little worried about whether or not they would be 'recognised' by anyone who might then take issue with what they had said or be put out in some way. The interviewees edited their interviews in such a way as to address these concerns. They and I also discussed, either face to face or over the phone, changes they wanted to make. Occasionally, it seemed to me that their editing was taking some of the specific flavour of the interview out of the text in favour of a smoother version of events. At the same time I could understand, and honoured of course, their desire to 'protect' others from their views, even if to me that did not always appear necessary. The final versions of the interviews were arrived at in consultation between the interviewees and myself, with the emphasis on their being satisfied with the text as it was in that version.

I enjoyed talking to the women very much. Their stories were all very different, which in itself is interesting. I was also struck by the ways in which doing Women's Studies was embedded in personal histories which could be read in very gendered ways. Their histories indicate why these women might be attracted to Women's Studies. Women's Studies addresses women. The very ambiguity of its title, suggesting both who is studying and what is being studied – women – makes women both the subject and the object of its enquiries. In one nifty move, it thus explodes the notion of a division between the knower and the known, inviting an equation which obliterates boundaries phallaciously (sic) taken for granted in many other disciplines. The fact that 'the personal is the political' constitutes one of the delights and one of the difficulties of Women's Studies, raising questions about how the personal is the political and what the implications of this are for Women's Studies as a discipline.

The phrase 'Women's Studies as a discipline' places it in the academy, and it is particularly in educational institutions which offer qualifications in Women's Studies that these questions arise. Once Women's Studies is aligned to other disciplines by virtue of being tied into degree and other institutional structures, it becomes answerable to a whole framework of references and requirements which can seem highly antagonistic to its concerns. Its claim to use personal experience as a resource, its rejection of particular modes of presentation and examination (specifically essays and three-hour unseen examinations) as the *only* valid ones for proving intellectual competence, its questioning of the idea of an objective and objectifiable notion of knowledge, its encouragement of women, frequently older women, to come into higher education institutions – all this does not necessarily endear it to the men who have dominated higher education, have tended to set its agendas and are, certainly in the 1990s, fighting and competing for ever-scarcer resources. Women are staking their claims.

The very androcentricity of education as it has been practised until recently, and still is, has encouraged many feminists to suggest that Women's Studies should make its space outside conventional higher education institutions. Many Women's Studies courses or related courses do take place outside the academy, and texts such as Jean Milloy and Rebecca O'Rourke's *The Woman Reader* and Sandra Butler and Claire Wintram's *Feminist Groupwork* discuss some such groups/courses. But change in the academy can be effected from within as well as from outside, and different educational contexts are likely to attract different groups of women. From that point of view, the more Women's Studies courses there are across a range of diverse settings, the better.

Women seek change when they come to Women's Studies courses and they are changed by attending such courses. The interviews in this book make this clear. But women change to the extent and in the ways that they want to or are prepared to change. You do not, for example, become a feminist or a lesbian against your will. You may not necessarily become either as a result of attending a Women's Studies course. You may be either or both before/without ever attending one. You may change in completely unexpected ways. Women's Studies enables women to deal with some of the queries they have about themselves and about other women.

This raises the issue of the role of personal experience in Women's Studies. Quite what role it has will depend on the context in which Women's Studies or related activities take place. You can have groups which function in therapeutic ways and where the sharing and analysing of personal experiences, akin to consciousness-raising groups, is the primary goal. On Women's Studies *degree courses*, whether at undergraduate or at postgraduate level, this is unlikely to be the case. Personal experience can and will be used on such courses, but the aim will be to integrate that material into a wider, more theorised frame which utilises critical and analytical reflection on experience, underpinned by knowledge of feminist theories and research. In an academic setting, the best feminist research is work that manages to construct an interface of personal experience and feminist theory. The essays in Section III below, by Women's Studies tutors working in different higher education institutions in Britain, discuss ways in which such work might be achieved without compromising a stance that is constructively self-critical as well as critical of the academy.

Although there have been Women's Studies courses in Britain for some years, it is still not necessarily the case that you will have encountered someone who does or has done Women's Studies. This accounts for why many women are vague about what Women's Studies is. Most of the women who teach Women's Studies today, including myself, were never themselves students on Women's Studies courses, although it is very likely that they have taught courses such as 'Women's Writing' or 'Gender and Society' or 'Women and the Law' as part of another discipline for a number of years. It is also likely that women teaching Women's Studies now have been feminists for a long time, were active in the Women's Liberation Movement of the late 1960s and 1970s, and are engaged in feminist activities outside the academy. We (meaning women teaching the subject) have probably become used to the idea of Women's Studies as a discipline, even though its parameters keep shifting and it still feels very much like the beginning.

However, the trajectories of women teaching Women's Studies now are likely to be somewhat different from those of women entering Women's Studies courses as students in the 1990s. If they are in their 20s in Britain, they will have lived virtually all their adult lives under a Conservative government and in a context in which confidence in any Women's Movement and in a universal sisterhood has given way to a recognition of the complexities of intrasexual differences. If they are older, they may or may not have engaged with the Women's Movement. Defining oneself as a feminist does not necessarily or unvaryingly come easily to women entering Women's Studies now. The 1990s are not the 1970s. There is thus a great diversity in the kinds of women who come to Women's Studies courses, and it is useful to be prepared for that and not to take for granted that every woman will know certain things or share particular positions.

References and Further Reading

Aaron, J. and S. Walby, eds (1991), *Out of the Margins: Women's Studies in the Nineties* (London: Falmer).

Abelove, H., M. A. Barale and D. M. Halperin, eds (1993), *The Lesbian and Gay Studies Reader* (London: Routledge).

Alcoff, L. and E. Potter, eds (1993), *Feminist Epistemologies* (London: Routledge).

Bannerji, H., L. Carty, K. Delhi, S. Heald, and K. McKenna, eds (1991), *Unsettling Relations: The University as a Site of Feminist Struggles* (Boston, MA: South End).

Berger Gluck, S. and D. Patai, eds (1991), *Women's Words: The Feminist Practice of Oral History* (London: Routledge).

Bowles, G. and R. Duelli Klein, eds (1983), *Theories of Women's Studies* (London: Routledge & Kegan Paul).

Bristol Women's Studies Group, eds (1979), *Half the Sky: An Introduction to Women's Studies* (London: Virago).

Butler, S. and C. Wintram (1991), *Feminist Groupwork* (London: Sage).

DuBois, E.C., G.P. Kelly, E. Kennedy Lapovsky, C.W. Korsmeyer and L.S. Robinson, eds (1985), *Feminist Scholarship: Kindling in the Groves of Academe* (Urbana: University of Illinois Press).

Griffin, G., M. Hester, S. Rai and S. Roseneil, eds (1994), *Stirring It: Challenges for Feminism.* (London: Falmer).

Gunew, S., ed.(1990), *Feminist Knowledge: Critique and Construct* (London: Routledge).

——, ed.(1991), *A Reader in Feminist Knowledge* (London: Routledge).

Hinds, H., A. Phoenix and J. Stacey, eds(1992), *Working Out: New Directions for Women's Studies* (London: Falmer).

Hull, G.T., P.B. Scott and B. Smith, eds (1982), *All the Women Are White, All the Men Are Black, But Some of Us Are Brave: Black Women's Studies* (New York: Feminist Press).

Humm, M., ed. (1992), *Feminisms: A Reader* (Hemel Hempstead: Harvester Wheatsheaf).

Jackson, S., *et al*, eds (1993), *Women's Studies: A Reader* (Hemel Hempstead: Harvester Wheatsheaf).

Kennedy, M., C. Lubelska and V. Walsh, eds (1993), *Making Connections: Women's Studies, Women's Movements, Women's Lives* (London: Falmer).

McDowell, L. and R. Pringle, eds (1992), *Defining Women* (Cambridge: Polity).

Milloy, J. and R. O'Rourke (1991), *The Woman Reader: Learning and Teaching Women's Writing* (London: Routledge).

Richardson, D. and V. Robinson, eds (1993), *Introducing Women's Studies* (London: Macmillan).

Stanley, L. and S. Wise (1993), *Breaking Out Again: Feminist Ontology and Epistemology*, 2nd edn. (London: Routledge).

Whitelegg, E., *et al*, eds (1982), *The Changing Experience of Women* (Oxford: Martin Robinson in association with the Open University).

Section I

The Experience of Women's Studies

1

The Desire for Change and the Experience of Women's Studies

GABRIELE GRIFFIN

Who Said It Was Simple

There are so many roots to the tree of anger
that sometimes the branches shatter
before they bear.

Sitting in Nedicks
the women rally before they march
discussing the problematic girls
they hire to make them free.
An almost white counterman passes
a waiting brother to serve them first
and the ladies neither notice nor reject
the slighter pleasures of their slavery.

But I who am bound by my mirror
as well as my bed
see cause in color
as well as sex.

and sit here wondering
which me will survive
all these liberations.

(1970)   (Audre Lorde)[1]

In my – partial – version of Audre Lorde's poem, the tree of anger, of which Adrienne Rich also writes 'that light of outrage is the light of history' (Rich 1991, p. 49), and seeing causes in sex is what fuels Women's Studies; the women rallying before they march are Women's Studies students having a coffee break together; the problematic girls (women, really) they hire are the Women's Studies tutors; and the I who wonders which me will survive all these liberations can be any of us.

I want to explore the desire for change which motivates women to enter a Women's Studies course. Women come to Women's

Studies in many different ways; some see courses – at whatever level – advertised or learn about them from friends, relations or colleagues; one woman told me that she was 'sold' a Women's Studies module when she came to an Open Day at her university where a tutor simply convinced her that this subject, which she had never heard of before, was just right for her. No matter how women arrive on Women's Studies courses, in some way or another they are motivated by the desire for change.

The Desire for Change

Desiring change in itself does not tell you about what kind of change you might want. In the first instance it simply registers the fact that you wish for alterations.

Definition
Who told me my place?
It takes generations
To breed such a true believer –
I am of the race
Of dutiful captives; it needed
Centuries, millenia, to produce
Someone who instinctively knew
The only movement possible
Was up or down:
...
But I am released by language,
I escape through speech:
Which has no dimensions,
Demands no local habitation
Or allegiance, which sets me free
From whomsoever's definition:
Jew, poet, woman.
                    (Ruth Fainlight)[2]

The desire for change can be quite non-specific and, indeed, even unconscious or inarticulate. Alternatively, you may have a very clear idea of what you want. You may want a further qualification, you may want to meet new people, you may want to improve your chances of getting a job or promotion, you may want to obtain a formal education which you have had no chance or opportunity to acquire before – or you may think that you are just interested in the subject Women's Studies, or what you imagine that subject is or will be about.

Clearly, all education is about change. As the origins of the word indicate, it is meant to 'lead [you] out of' whatever it is you are in. Additionally, and this is quite important, education is a by and large *socially sanctioned* means of effecting change; if you want change and you are either clear that you want a degree, or not too certain what it is you want, education is an obvious and generally approved way of pursuing change, whether through evening classes, Saturday schools, Access courses or degree courses.

Different Women/Diverse Agendas

Women come into Women's Studies for a variety of reasons. Moreover, any one woman will probably have not just one but several agendas. These agendas may be personal, educational, professional or social. They can reach quite a long way back into an individual woman's history or may be very recent. Many women I spoke to whose interviews are transcribed below located their coming to Women's Studies in a past in which they had experienced themselves as disadvantaged, where they had been, as one woman put it, treated as 'second-class citizens' within their own families, or had experienced similar disadvantages at school or in their jobs precisely because – and this was often made unashamedly explicit – they are women. This can then mean that a woman decides to do Women's Studies because she expects to be on an equal footing with the other women on such a course, as they, too, are women and as the subject is *Women*'s Studies. Or she may want to prove to herself, and possibly to others, that she is capable of doing such a course.

If an agenda of attempting to understand how being a woman has conditioned one's experiences is top of the list for some women, others may want to advance professionally by getting a particular qualification, with the subject in which that qualification is obtained appearing to be of secondary importance. (Not all Women's Studies courses lead to a qualification – many have no particular qualifications attached to them.) Yet other women may want to join Women's Studies because they remember fondly previous experiences they had in all-women's groups – experiences that may date back to the 1970s and early 1980s when women's consciousness-raising groups existed, offering women the much-needed space in which to articulate their experiences and desires.[3]

No matter what are the agenda(s) of any individual woman for entering Women's Studies, meeting other women who seem to have different priorities from oneself can be quite an experience: overwhelming, disappointing, surprising or something else entirely. When I talked to women about their expectations of the other people they would meet on the course, their responses fell broadly into three categories:

1.   Some had no particular expectation of what other women in Women's Studies might be like.
2.   Some expected the other women to be very like themselves.
3.   Some thought the other women would be very different from themselves.

No Expectations

Having no expectation of what other women coming on a Women's Studies course will be like can be useful in terms of preserving an openness towards others, which may also mean that you will not be subject to disappointment on account of other women not being what you expected them to be. This can be very helpful. But having no expectations can be due to other stances than simple openness. It may, for example, be a function of not having a very clear idea of what the subject is about (a position which is actually quite common among prospective students of Women's Studies); or of not having a very strong sense of social needs in relation to the course, meaning that you do not come to the course with the explicit expectation or hope of making friends on the course. It may be that you've had bad experiences on other courses and therefore do not want to come with specific expectations of people. One thing is for certain: if you really have no expectations of what the other women on the course will be like, or you do not 'allow' yourself to have such expectations, you will be surprised by the women you encounter, because you have not imagined them before.

Like Me

You will also be surprised by the women on the course if you expect them to be like you (an expectation which, I found, a consider-able number of women have), because the chances are *they won't be*. That does not mean that you will not find them interesting in ways you had not anticipated, but it does mean that you have to revise your fantasy about other women on the course in the light of the reality that you find. Expecting others to be like oneself, or to want the same things out of a Women's Studies course, is a narcissistic fallacy, expressive of the desire to find someone just like oneself.

Many women I spoke to expected other women on the course to be like themselves in very specific ways. For instance, they expected their co-students to have come on the course for the same reason(s) they themselves had done so. They expected others to be, or not to be, feminists if they themselves were/not. They expected others to want to socialize and share things. They expected strong commitment to the subject. They expected ... The list could go on. If they had come wanting a particular degree, for example, but found that others on the course had come in order to explore aspects of their personal selves, this needed some negotiation. Encountering women with diverse agendas and negotiating these differences is thus one of the challenges on Women's Studies courses.

Unlike Me

This is also the case if women come with expectations that the other women on a Women's Studies course will be unlike them. Quite a few women said to me that they joined such a course in the *hope* of meeting women unlike themselves, which again is an expression of a desire for change. Some women want to be challenged, to encounter someone new and different in order to enable them to rethink their own position. A good example of this is Gina, one of the women I interviewed, an older, card-carrying Tory who expected and hoped that the Women's Studies course would be, as she put it, a 'lesbian, left-wing hornets' nest'.

Others may simply see themselves as 'different' from other women and want that difference confirmed in the women they meet on the course. Yet others may wish to meet kinds of women whom they do not appear to encounter in their everyday lives; women, perhaps, who embody what they might want to be like, role models for or exemplars of a different lifestyle from their own.

Most women who expect other women on a Women's Studies course to be very different from themselves find that the others are not as different as they hoped or thought. Why, after all, should others be normatively different? The truth is that a vast range of very different women attend Women's Studies courses, that they are not a homogeneous group, that their views may differ sharply or slightly on certain issues but that, for most of the time, these women are as diverse as any group of women is going to be. The dominant shared characteristic is likely to be that all the women want change in some way and that all of them hope to achieve it through Women's Studies.

To Be or Not to Be a Feminist

One very important expectation some women have of other women in Women's Studies is that they too will be feminists. Due to the very women-centredness of Women's Studies, one might expect all women in the field to declare themselves feminists, but this is far from being the case. Many women, particularly when they first start on Women's Studies courses, have no overt investment in feminism at all. Their view of feminism is informed by the caricatures of feminists as bra-burning, man-hating, dungaree-wearing, shaven-headed (or very nearly so) that have been the delight and weapon of those afraid of women claiming themselves, a space of their own, equal rights, a voice. It is a sign of the persistence of this anxiety, of the backlash[4] against the advances women have made in improving *some* of the conditions under which we live, that those caricatures continue to inhabit people's, including some women's, imagination.

Women's fear of feminism stems partly from a fear of being identified with the caricatures of feminists that are an aspect of the public imagination.[5] Such identification, women rightly surmise, will make them 'outsiders' in many contexts, may alienate them from those people with whom they spend large parts of their lives, professionally, socially, personally. This is because feminism is constructed as opposing men, patriarchy, femininity, the power structures which dictate that you make the tea while he pinches your bum. And of course feminism does oppose all these things, though not, perhaps, in quite the way(s) people may expect. However, even if an individual woman feels uncomfortable with some or all of these things, the chances are that she has, and has been encouraged to, invested in them so heavily that to articulate her discomfort would also imply an extensive questioning of what she has been doing until she reaches that point of articulation. So it can be a lot less threatening to let things go, to accept how she is treated in the name of 'peace'; her own peace as well as that of others. To quote from Aspen's poem 'For My "Apolitical" Sisters':[6]

listen:
oppression is not a choice
or just the misfortune of the socially deprived
no woman has escaped
sexism falls like quiet rain
constantly, softly seeping in
until we all become saturated
and it gently, ever so gently
so we hardly notice
does us terrible violence ...

It is very important to remember how incredibly hard it is not only to shift your perceptions but to voice them, to offer resistance to what is the 'norm', however degrading it may be to yourself, if you are in an environment where nobody supports your stance, where everybody else thinks it is OK for men to dictate the terms and for women to take them down. Women who are feminists and identify themselves as such publicly often feel able to do so because they live in environments where others are either sympathetic to their position, or at least would not publicly and/or directly question the validity of feminism. If as a vegetarian you spend all your time with other vegetarians it becomes difficult to imagine what it is like to be the only vegetarian among meat-and-two-veg eaters. Similarly, if as a feminist you live and work among people whose attitudes towards feminism range from sympathetic to indifferent, it becomes hard to imagine what it is like to try and be a feminist in an entirely misogynistic environment.

This does not detract from the disappointment some women, particularly women with a history of involvement in feminist activities, feel on encountering other women in Women's Studies who reject the label 'feminist' and manifest a hostility towards it which one might expect only from very reactionary men. But individual histories differ; understanding that difference, coming to terms with the fact that many women on Women's Studies courses *now* were toddlers during the 1960s and early 1970s when the Women's Liberation Movement was in its heyday, and that many women lived through the years of that movement as teenagers and adults without directly encountering or seeking out its manifestations, is one of the tasks of Women's Studies and every woman within it. It is crucial in the face of this diversity to surface and debate the engagements and investments different women have made in relation to their positions – the worst counterscenario is the one where different groups of women simply refuse to engage with each other.

> Silence can be a plan
> rigorously executed
>
> the blueprint of life
> It is a presence
> it has a history   a form
>
> Do not confuse it
> with any kind of absence
>   (Adrienne Rich)[7]

The Willingness to Engage

Willingness to engage and debate may be a function of the desire to persuade the other person of the 'rightness' of your own position, but it also signals an openness to hearing the other's point of view. That openness is not easy to achieve; it implies vulnerability, lays you open to the possibility of a change in your position. Such change, if desired, can be exhilarating; if feared, it can be very threatening. For change, whether desired or feared, indicates a questioning of the position you have adopted until that point; after all, you would not want to change it if it was entirely satisfactory.

The admission that you would like to change something thus undermines the stability of what you have had until then. What you have had is no longer exactly what you want, or is no longer 'enough'. The implication seems to be that there is something wrong with how things were before you decided to embark on a change, that you are rewriting what was until the point of change and revaluing it – in negative terms. It may of course simply be the case that you want something *different*, not necessarily better or worse. Wanting change is a recognition of the fact that all people change over time.

Desiring change offers comment not only on your hopes for the future but also on what you had in the past. Questioning the past is a very brave thing to do, and not easy to accommodate. The past, after all, is, as many say, the only certainty we have; to question it is to allow a large dose of uncertainty to enter one's consciousness. If you have spent many years taking it for granted that your primary duty is to your husband and your children, putting yourself first can be incredibly difficult. If you believe that changing the laws pertaining to the labour market will give women equality in the workplace, you will find it difficult not to see women who have suffered unequal treatment at work as the exception rather than the norm. If you think of women as 'naturally' nurturant and caring, you will find it hard to see violent women as anything but 'bad' or, more likely, 'mad'. Coming out of a context in which women automatically take second place makes it very difficult to put them first. If you have spent most of your time conforming to the demands of heteropatriarchy, it is hard to rethink that.

However, it is not only the individual woman on a Women's Studies course who is affected in this way – her actions will have reverberations among friends, colleagues and relations. You cannot initiate change in your own life without that affecting others. This is an important point which one can easily overlook or not anticipate.

If you are attending a course, any course, you need time – for starters. Time to attend the course and time to work for it. If the course is tied to a qualification, the demand to spend time working for it becomes perhaps even greater. This time will have to come from somewhere. If you have or develop a commitment to the course, you will no longer be available to other people in the same way as you were before you started the course. If the people around you are supportive of you and your endeavours, they will help you to free up time, by taking over jobs from/for you and such like. They will recognise and accept your need to develop your self in the way you have chosen.

It is equally likely that your attending a course can foster resentment, especially if you live with a partner and/or children used to having you at their disposal. Women's socialisation into other-orientation, into putting others first, can then mean that the woman taking time to do a course begins to and/or is made to feel guilty. She tries to do everything and, inevitably, finds herself either completely exhausted or unable to do justice to it all, so that she herself will start to develop feelings of resentment. Negotiating between your own and others' needs can become a major issue when attending a course.

Why do *Women's* Studies?

If this course happens to be a Women's Studies course, such negotiations can be particularly difficult. A woman doing a

Women's Studies course is likely to face questions about the validity of that course. 'Why do *Women*'s Studies?'[8] will be a question she may encounter more times than she cares to answer it. The question usually carries one or several subtexts or subquestions, which often enough explicitly surfaced. These may include: 'Are you a lesbian?',[9] 'What's Women's Studies?',[10] 'What's the point of doing anything with "women" in the title?' For the woman beginning Women's Studies these can be quite daunting questions; she may feel fairly clear about whether or not she is a lesbian, but she may well find it difficult to answer questions about the validity of Women's Studies, academic or otherwise, and she may not be too sure of her own or other women's worth *as women*, especially if she has spent much time in a context where she has experienced being put down for being a woman as a virtually automatic response.

One of the tasks of Women's Studies, which, as a discipline, is still fighting for and needing to justify its claim to space in the academy,[11] is to enable women to develop a sense of self-worth *as women*, to acquire the arguments to articulate the importance of women and of Women's Studies, and to understand why some people react negatively to the whole concept.

As part of this it is important to realise that the question 'Why do *Women*'s Studies?' is *never* asked in a disinterested manner. Indeed, some of the problems in answering this question arise precisely because of this. In answering this question women often feel compelled to address the subtexts raised by the question, subtexts that need to be understood as an expression of the questioner's anxiety about change. To answer the question, it is therefore often not enough to say that we live in a misogynistic society in which women are systematically and overtly disadvantaged – though that is certainly the case. In Britain, we can cite the legal position of female prostitutes, the operations of the recently established Child Support Agency, the government campaign rounding on single mothers, the church's difficulty in accepting the ordination of women, and many more examples to reveal how systematically inequality between the sexes is built into our society's structures. But that is not enough, for the counterargument is frequently either, 'But you are not one of them,' meaning you are not one of the obviously disadvantaged, or, 'Women can do anything now. Look at Margaret Thatcher.' But one nameable woman does not make for equality.

Understanding the barriers that create tokenism is important. The fact that in theory women may be able to 'do anything' does not detract from the deeply ingrained expectations that when childcare needs sorting out or a child is sick at home, the mother rather than her partner will take care of this situation, or that having a Black face will automatically lower your chances of getting a job. Here's the experience of one Black woman:

> I completed the course [touch-typing] and tried to find a job. It wasn't easy. After numerous 'we'll let you know's and direct 'no's I realized for the first time that the main reason for these rejections was that I was black. I think it was the first time I'd experienced direct racism. I registered with every office agency and was unsuccessful with all of them. (McNeill *et al*, pp. 21–2)

The schools you attended may have channelled you towards doing subjects that are supposed to be 'suitable for girls', operating in such a way as to make it difficult for you to develop a career. You may have made, and may have been encouraged by friends, family and conventions to make, choices, personal and profes-sional, that have all said, '*Because I am a female* I do x' – for instance, become a secretary, do unskilled part-time labour, stay at home with the children, expect to get married after finishing my education.

These pressures to conform to an image of femininity encap-sulated in how women are treated and represented (helpless, in need of male support, assertive and independent but waiting for Mr Right, etc.) are real and sometimes insurmountable barriers for women to climb over if they desire change.

The people they are closest to may resist their desire for change. As Kate Hevner Mueller puts it:

> [c]onflict between the sexes is inevitable whenever customary roles and statuses are threatened. In this case it is the man's earning capacity, his political power, his freedom of opportunity, his monopoly on the places of eminence, that are now being challenged by women. (Hevner Mueller 1954, p. 57)

Women on Women's Studies courses have fathers, brothers, male lovers and partners, sons, male friends and acquaintances, male bosses – men with whom they have formed allegiances and part-nerships, whom they do not necessarily or obviously experience as oppressive,[12] on whom they are frequently emotionally and economically dependent, and with whom they are likely to spend more time than they will ever spend attending a Women's Studies seminar. Understanding this is crucial to understanding why women may come to Women's Studies against enormous odds and why they may be reluctant to call themselves feminists. It is also crucial that one takes into account the possibility of such commitments when one begins to engage with the fact that all women are not the same as oneself, do not share the same perceptions and positions. As Judith Barrington puts it:[13]

> Where are the brave new worlds
> I have heard about
> and dreamed about with you?
> There for the taking, if only
> roots and strands and
> great enormous burrowing growths
> of old familiar worlds
> were not embedded deep within me.

Pointing out the manifest inequalities between the sexes in our society provides one reason, perhaps the major one, for the existence of Women's Studies, which as a discipline seeks to address, analyse and counter these inequalities; but if used as an argument to 'defend' Women's Studies, this can serve to reinforce partners' or colleagues' anxiety about you becoming politically and personally radicalised by such a course. Awareness might breed resistance, after all. In this context, another course of action might be the attempt to engage directly with people's anxieties, to ask them, 'How do you *feel* about my doing Women's Studies?'; 'What is it about this course that makes you anxious/ aggressive/defensive?'; 'What do you imagine might be the consequence of my doing the course/becoming more feminist?' Giving others some space to voice their concerns, at the same time as understanding that these are *their concerns* and addressing them as such, may help others to come to terms with your desires for change. Unless you keep completely quiet about Women's Studies, not only will you encounter questioning, but others with whom you spend time may have to engage in a process of reviewing and rethinking as well.

Here it is important to bear in mind that it may not be men or *only* men who resist the desire for change that a woman is signalling by attending a Women's Studies course. Female friends and colleagues will react too – with delight or with dismay. Again, the point is that by manifesting a desire for change, a woman raises questions about her situation up till that point – and, by implication, she raises questions about the situation of others around her. If *she* is dissatisfied with what she has had, if *she* is seeking change, maybe *I* should do the same, maybe *my* life is not what it should be.

Understanding the threat others may feel when one is making changes oneself is important for trying to preserve relationships that are significant in one's life. Naturally, one can simply deny that going on a Women's Studies course will make a difference; indeed some women coming on to such courses either start out with the hope that attending the course will not imply changes or, finding that it might, decide not to take up these possibilities for change. One woman I interviewed who emphatically did not regard herself as a feminist said to me: 'I hope to change – after all, that's what education is for – but not so much that my family and friends won't recognise me.'

Yet another strategy for dealing with other people's anxieties about your attending a Women's Studies course is not to be defensive or to deny the possibility of its impact but to affirm that you want something new, a change, and you would like others – but do not necessarily expect them to do so – to share that desire. It can actually feel really good to say, 'I *want* to do the course,' and, 'I think I'll *enjoy* thinking about women and our situation in society.' Affirming one's decisions, one's desire for change, saying 'Yes,' can be enormously self-empowering.

Women's Studies: Claiming Space

In the first instance, Women's Studies is about women claiming space for themselves. This is nothing new or specific to Women's Studies.[14] In Western society there are many women's spaces, from the 'Ladies' to 'hen' parties and nunneries, from sex-segregated wards in hospitals and changing rooms in shops to Women's Institute groups. But these spaces tend to be *allocated* to, rather than taken by, women; they also frequently serve to support rather than to question gender-stereotyping. In the academy, however – and I accept that many Women's Studies courses do not take place there – women are still peripheral, even though they dominate (at least at undergraduate level) certain subject areas, specifically arts and humanities subjects. But, as Saul Feldman unflinchingly puts it: 'Like female-dominated occupations, female-dominated academic disciplines are low in prestige, low in economic rewards, and low in power' (Feldman 1974, p. 46).

Women's low status in the academy persists, as does the reflexive devaluation of what women do. As suggested above, this needs to be seen not in terms of the actual worth of what women do but in terms of the gendered power structures which inform our society and the anxiety concerning their erosion that it expresses. Women claiming space in the academy thus may be read either as the grit getting into the oyster, or as the virus entering the body. An element foreign to the academy[15] is introduced when women claim space within it, immediately raising the question: what will happen to the body which hosts them? Can it stay the same? Will it change? Will it transform? Will it die?

It is interesting here to consider Women's Studies as a discipline in relation to what Oliver Fulton in 1989 described as the dominant model of British higher education (a model which of course has changed in some respects now, and which is particularly pertinent to undergraduate rather than to postgraduate education). Fulton lists the following as the chief traits of British higher education:

- an insistence on standard forms of knowledge and certification on entry;
- entry immediately after school;
- a period of study lasting for three or four years full time, but with long vacations and a considerable amount of spare time during term;
- study away from the (parental) home, preferably taking up residence within the institution, and relatively isolated from the surrounding community;
- study leading to a degree, preferably a specialized honours degree;
- study based on and within 'disciplines', which may have little relevance to the student's prior or subsequent experience;
- the use of expert/novice forms of teaching, exemplified by the lecture and the three-hour unseen written examination, and sustained by the notion of a body of knowledge which has to be mastered;
- the majority of the costs incurred borne by the state and the student's parents. (Fulton, 1989, p. 91)

In comparing these characteristics with Women's Studies (and, to be fair, not all of them apply to other 'disciplines' or to all education institutions any more), it becomes instantly obvious how far removed from the dominant model of British higher education Women's Studies is. Thus there is no insistence on standard forms of knowledge and certification on entry – there is no demand for 'A' levels or similar qualifications as the *only* way of entering a Women's Studies course. 'Non-standard entrants' has now become a frequently used phrase in education; one which, for all its discriminatory implications, flags up a change in what used to be the norm.

Many women, as this book makes clear in the interviews section, do not come to Women's Studies immediately from school; a large number of students are older women who may have had a considerable number of years away from education. Study time on Women's Studies courses varies enormously, depending on what kind of a course it is; today there are probably more students engaged in Women's Studies courses which are atypical in terms of Fulton's model than those that are typical of it. This is because there are more postgraduate courses and courses operating in Adult Education and the Workers' Educational Association (WEA) on Women's Studies than there are undergraduate courses. Many of the latter, in any event, now follow a modular structure, so that the amount of time a student studies Women's Studies even at undergraduate level can vary tremendously from institution to institution.

Many Women's Studies students, often precisely because they are 'mature', with family and job commitments, tend to study in their home town, never taking up residence in the institution and remaining strongly embedded in their local community. They may be studying for a degree, but this is not necessarily so. Moreover, women who are on Women's Studies courses leading to degrees often say that they would do the course even if there was no degree attached to it at the end. One of the major strengths and distinguishing traits of Women's Studies as a discipline is that it makes and encourages the explicit use of students' experiences, which are regarded as a resource. Its interdisciplinarity or multidisciplinarity threatens conventional conceptions of 'single' disciplines, the idea of 'the expert' and 'specialism', and the very territorialities which inform academe.[16]

Women's Studies courses tend to use interactive learning methods which break down the binary divide between teacher and student. Instead they build through team-teaching, group work and discussion, encouraging students to participate and to articulate their positions. Many Women's Studies courses use neither lectures (certainly not hour-long lectures) nor three-hour unseen examinations as their methods of instilling and testing learning. Many are assessed in terms of coursework, and the kinds of coursework which are encouraged go far beyond the essay format commonly demanded of undergraduates. And the cost of attending Women's Studies courses is overwhelmingly borne by the students themselves.

If I look at the MA in Women's Studies which I am involved with, and compare it to the MA in Modern English Studies on which I also teach, as well as with my own experiences as an undergraduate and postgraduate, what strikes me most about Women's Studies, certainly at postgraduate level, is that it brings into that sector of education a clientele that has been, and still for the most part is, excluded from that educational space. The vast majority of postgraduates is (still) male; most are fresh from their first degree. This is not so in Women's Studies where, on many courses, women aged 30 and over form the majority of students. Basically, Women's Studies has introduced a new type of student into the academy.

This also means that there are a number of women on Women's Studies courses who are given the opportunity to acquire a certain educational training that they did not have when they were younger. Additionally, women doing Women's Studies is a sign of the increasing 'professionalisation' of many jobs dominated by women, such as (often the lower ranks of) the health and social services, as well as the fact that certain educational sectors now require more and more qualifications of their staff and thus encourage women to do degrees. While this is in some respects enabling to women as individuals, one also has to put this development into an economic and political perspective and recognise that Women's Studies has not arrived in educational institutions without the support of governmental and educational bodies with vested and specific interests. These are not driven by the goodness of their patriarchal hearts but by the recognition that women play an increasingly prominent role in the workforce, and that their education is of crucial importance for the twenty-first century. On one level Women's Studies is thus a way of bringing women into the fold, offering them space in (frequently) mainstream establishments in order to educate and (thus) incorporate the resource they represent.

Institutionally, women gain visibility through the presence of Women's Studies courses and through students who are, for the most part, not necessarily visible on all other courses. Taking into account the needs of women students in terms of library resources, opening hours, crèche facilities, safer rides home, measures changes in the culture of an institution. Consideration of women's needs may be alien to that culture; what women do and how they are assumed to be may be the subject of avuncular derision or hostility, but the mere fact of the necessity to engage with women students' needs carves out a space for women in institutional consciousness. What is more, in the cost-counting 1990s women are a source of revenue and have to be reckoned with institutionally because they represent economic power and hence institutional income; a fact that, once realised, can be a very empowering experience for women, never mind the institution.

Dealing with Difference

'Difference' has become a key term in Women's Studies.[17] But the history of the change in Women's Studies from a focus on commonalities among women to a recognition of and engagement with their differences from one another is known chiefly to those who have either been engaged in Women's Studies and/or feminist activism for some considerable time, or to women who, due to an active interest in the subject, have read around it. Women new to Women's Studies in the 1990s may not as a matter of course have thought about difference other than the differences between women and men.

Some differences are more immediately visible than others. Differences that register on the surface of the body are more obviously noticeable than those that are not. We may note the colour of a woman or whether or not she has a disability, but we may not be aware of her sexuality or her class. So we tend to make assumptions – when someone appears different from ourselves, we expect them to be different; when somebody appears to be the same, we treat them as similar to ourselves.[18] Any of these stances is of course informed by prejudice, and can lead to inadvertent or deliberate moves to include or exclude the woman we experience as different. For example, as a mother one may assume that every other woman in the group is also a mother and therefore very interested or not at all interested in children, as the case may be. Such an assumption fails to take into account that there are women in the group who are not mothers. Or we may present ourselves as 'coupled' women, forgetting that some women are single. We may 'require' the person whom we perceive to be different because she is Black[19] or lesbian[20] or has a disability[21] to be the representative of the group to which we assign her, making her the 'expert' on sexuality or ethnicity or dis/ability without considering our own positions in all this. A very clear example of this kind of problem occurred recently in a Women's Studies session where the one Black woman present began to voice her concerns over representations of women from diverse ethnic backgrounds and how these representations always serve to problematise Black women. Another, white, student leapt in and began to say that this was hardly surprising given the issue of clitoridectomies, with which she disagreed. In that instant it was clear that the white woman in question was completely unaware she was reproducing precisely the stereotyping which the Black woman had sought to highlight. The ensuing discussion brought to the surface the difficulties of dealing with differences among women without reproducing the value systems in which they are – often negatively – embedded.

I am reminded of a poem by Jean Binta Breeze:[22]

Mother ... Sister ... Daughter ...
'If you should see me,
walking down the street,
mouth muffled
head low against the wind,
know
that this is no woman bent
on sacrifice
just
heavy
with the thoughts
of freedom ...'

Negotiating difference, without making the other person the different one, the one who has to bear the burden of difference, is very difficult and needs constant practice as well as constant openness to challenging one's own position. By making others experts, we may end up silencing ourselves; by seeing ourselves as the experts, we may silence other women.

Experiencing Difference

Experiencing the burden of difference can be intensely disempowering. You may feel that you have nothing in common with the women you encounter on the Women's Studies course. Many of the women I talked to mentioned their sense of (academic) inadequacy. They had come with a history of not doing well in other educational settings, of not being encouraged to think of themselves as academically competent, of having been put down as a 'stupid girl', of having been required to relinquish their studies to look after others or when the money ran out (which it tends to do more for girls than boys), of not being allowed or not having allowed themselves to achieve academically.

Such lack of confidence was regarded by some as the reason for choosing Women's Studies rather than a different subject, sometimes because they expected a supportive all-female environment on such a course, and sometimes because they thought that Women's Studies would enable them to utilise what they did know something about – women's situation in society – rather than confronting them with a completely unfamiliar and seemingly extrinsic body of knowledge, foreign to themselves and their experiences.

Lack of confidence and low self-esteem could thus be converted into their opposites through the encouragement in Women's Studies to investigate what one knows and to view that not as an isolated case but as a part of a general socially and culturally constructed phenomenon. Liberation can be found in the sheer knowledge that one is not alone in one's experiences. One woman interviewed below, for instance, said to me that finding out that other women experience men as compartmentalising their lives – to the detriment of women who find themselves horned into shoe boxes, waiting to be taken out for whatever purpose is assigned to them and then put back again until the next time – was very reassuring. In her view, knowing that she was not the only one who experienced things in those terms enabled her to stop regarding this perception as in some way *her* problem.

While finding out that you are not 'the only one' is probably one of the best experiences a woman can have on a Women's Studies course, finding out that you *are* 'the only one' can be very difficult. What do you do if you are the only Black woman or the only lesbian on a course full of white and heterosexual women? Whether or not your difference is visible, you have to decide what position to adopt. Should you come out? Should you bring your difference into play? Should you raise the issue of race? When? How? Or, indeed, should it be up to *you* rather than anyone else involved in the course to address difference? What moves you decide to make will depend on your history and your perception of the others around you. If they appear to be sympathetic to you and to issues of difference, you may feel comfortable about

57280

'coming out'. If not, you may sit back and wait to see how things will develop.

The others on the course are probably doing the same. As women, often objects in situations where we do not experience ourselves as in control, it can be very hard to see that we also set the agenda, that we, too, are involved in determining what happens. We can take action. We can take responsibility for initiating an engagement with difference. We can help set the agenda for how it is dealt with. We are not without power. And we need to realise this and act accordingly. Often. Only when we practise how to initiate action, take some responsibility for setting agendas and offer our perceptions for discussions can we gain the confidence to do so and learn how we can live with our differences. To quote Adrienne Rich's 'For Memory':[23]

> I can't know what you know
> unless you tell me
> there are gashes in our understandings
> of this world
> We came together in a common
> fury of direction
> barely mentioning difference
> ...
> The past is not a husk   yet change goes on ...

The Knower and the Known

Women's Studies is unlike other disciplines because, as its very title makes clear, it addresses a specific constituency of people – women. In quasi-narcissistic fashion, it therefore also automatically draws women as its audience. This is not a trait specific to Women's Studies but inherent in the effect all labels have on those who encounter them – they function to include and to exclude. To the extent that we feel included, we may be attracted to or repelled by what the label seems to denote. The description 'Fascist Tea Party' would, after all, be unlikely to encourage the same kinds of people to attend as one advertised as a 'New Men's Co-Counselling Session'.

The label 'Women's Studies' thus predominantly attracts women, as they, in all their diversity, are directly addressed by the title. This often comes out in how women talk about the desire to attend a Women's Studies course. They make comments such as: 'I thought this course would have something to do with *me*,' or, 'I feel that I can contribute to this course because it's about me.' They also often say: 'I am doing this course for myself,' or, 'I want to do this course because it has nothing to do with anything else I do.' All of these remarks in different ways testify to the ways in which women make direct connections between themselves and Women's Studies courses.

It is one of the distinguishing traits of Women's Studies that it addresses women directly, that it is about and for women. Unlike other subjects which mask what the relationship is between knower and knowledge, Women's Studies overtly sets up women both as the subjects (the knowers) and the objects (the knowledge) of its enquiry. Women's Studies provides a context in which women look at themselves and other women. They are simultaneously subjects and objects.

This generates both one of the joys and one of the difficulties of Women's Studies. It explodes the idea that knowledge is outside of and independent from the self, a notion which forms the basis of much conventional academic enquiry and allows students and teachers alike to take the position that whatever it is you are engaged with has 'nothing to do with you', does not affect or effect you in any (significant) way. By contrast, the very simultaneity of being both the subject and the object of Women's Studies means that everything is personal as well as political, that it is not possible to dissociate yourself from what you encounter.

This is one of the hardest lessons of Women's Studies. Recently when I talked with a group of Women's Studies students one turned to me and said, 'Women's Studies courses ought to carry a government health warning.' She went on to explain that she had not expected the course to have as profound an effect on her as it was having; after only four weeks, she was changing her own teaching elsewhere to take account of what she had been learning, and as for the way she was having to rethink her personal life … Initially, she said, she had been quite depressed by this, but she was beginning to feel different, empowered, much more positive. It turned out that she had been helped in regaining her equilibrium by talking with other students on the course, discovering that they were going through similar reactions.

As already suggested, it is one of the consequences of education that change occurs and that this change will effect change in one's environment. But with Women's Studies, the experience of that change may be more dramatic than with other subjects, simply because Women's Studies makes explicit the relationship between knower and knowledge.

Making this connection explicit can be very liberating. I love the (in this context very appropriate) opening lines of one of Judith Barrington's poems:[24]

> A million marching women
> each with a mirror in her hand
> laying bare her bowels
> in an orgy of self-realization.

For one thing, this connection between knower and knowledge provides women with an opportunity to explore themselves and their experiences and to see them in relation to other women's experiences as well as in diverse theoretical feminist frameworks. This can be a tremendous source of support, providing women with an affirmation of their existence and importance. I was very impressed by the story of a Black woman I talked to who said that she had been embarrassed to admit where she came from because nobody had ever heard of the island where she had been born. Going on a course that dealt with women in the Caribbean had taught her about the women of her island and had made her feel proud to come from there. Another woman spoke of the humiliation and degradation she had experienced when subjected to gynaecological inspections; she said that understanding the androcentricity of the medical world and how women's bodies were constructed within medical discourses had enabled her to put her own experiences in a context which depersonalised what had happened. Again, this is very important: to the extent that women are not used to and are not encouraged to think and speak about their experiences, they tend to regard these as 'private' and 'personal', and with that, very often, as somehow 'their fault' or 'their peculiarity' or 'their problem'. It is precisely the deprivatisation of experience, the assertion that the personal is the political, which can enable women to unburden themselves of notions of personal insufficiency and guilt.

However, it is also the case that understanding the personal as political is experienced as intensely threatening by some women. A woman, married, with children and a job, may have come on a course for reasons that may or may not be very clear to her, to find that the things she has taken for granted, such as her marriage, her role as mother, her job, come under a scrutiny which asks her to revalue the roles she has inhabited. Or a young woman, newly in love with her boyfriend, may find herself involved in a discussion which suggests that all heterosexual intercourse is oppressive to women.[25] If you have always, and basically unquestioningly, done the chores at home, it can be quite destabilising to have it suggested to you that this indicates your oppression in the domestic sphere.[26]

Not all women find it easy to cope with the ways in which Women's Studies asks them to engage with their selves. There are many things which we have good reasons to want to forget or not to confront, such as sexual coercion, (the memory of) physical and/or psychological violence done to us, or how we have been denigrated at school and at work, which may evoke our sense of helplessness, powerlessness, shame or guilt. We may still feel all these things and, what is more, we may suffer the memories of experiences we feel we cannot undo because they are in the past. We may not want to look at how that past still affects our present, still makes us act and react in ways that were set up possibly long before we were adults.

More than that, we may fear change. We may have gone through too much change to be able to face more, or we may have gone through too few changes to be able to imagine that we can survive change, and possibly even come out better. Or we may have had very bad experiences of trying to effect change, only to find that we ended up worse than before. But there are also women who have made changes and have learnt to accommodate and survive them, and who feel that their lives have improved as a result of allowing change to happen. It is from all these different women that we can learn, and the deprivatisation of experience helps that process.

Some Actualities Affecting Women's Studies Courses

Because Women's Studies addresses women directly, and because it explodes the notion of a separation of knower from knowledge, women come to Women's Studies with heightened expectations. Whether these are fully articulated or have not been raised to the surface of consciousness, they inform our experience of the course. I would argue that it is generally the case that one's expectations of an educational experience never quite match the reality one encounters on a course. That is because our fantasy of what that experience might be like is unmediated by the reality of the course. Hopes and fears alike are in that sense self-generated and self-referential.

The encounter with others encourages us to modify our perceptions, to rethink our desires in the light of their reality. The initial reaction to this is quite likely to be one of disappointment. Other women are not like you expected them to be. What you imagined and what actually happens on the course turn out to be two separate things. The reading you have to do may be more than you expected. Others may be less forthcoming in their views than you had hoped for. Topics you wanted to cover are not touched upon. You may not feel able to participate in discussions as you might wish. At the same time, you are likely to find that Women's Studies offers you issues to consider that you had never thought of, enables you to meet and find that you can work with and like women whom you would never encounter or choose to meet in your day-to-day existence.

Learning to deal with the gap between desire and reality, between your fantasy of the course and the reality of it, is crucial to your experience of the course. That also means coming to terms with the constraints under which we all operate and which we do not take into account in our fantasies. These include realising the amount of commitment that embarking on a Women's Studies course means, attempting to attend every week even in the face of other demands on you, living with other people's reactions to you doing the course, coping with working on coursework to deadlines, dealing with libraries and resources everybody else also wants access to, handling the fact that you may have assignments and that you may do well and/or not so well in these, understanding other women's needs on the course and learning that your own needs will not inevitably be met, and so forth. These are all quite difficult things to negotiate, especially as they have to be faced again and again, rather than on a one-off basis.

Women's Studies courses are subject to many constraints, such as *institutional* ones, ones to do with the staff and ones to do with the students themselves. Institutionally, the courses may suffer from material constraints like under-resourcing, lack of funds for library provision, or inadequate facilities in terms of rooms in which the courses take place. They may also be the subject of ideological conflicts, both within the course itself and outside it. If the courses lead to specific academic qualifications, these may demand that the student do coursework or examinations that run counter to the ways in which knowledge is constructed in Women's Studies, requiring competition, particular ways of presenting knowledge, particular ways of arguing points and so on. It is for these reasons that many feminists have maintained that Women's Studies can only operate outside established academic institutions.

Among the *constraints on staff* that may affect their work on Women's Studies courses are institutional imperatives such as ensuring that specific academic standards are maintained, and working within existing resources and restrictions governing these (you cannot, for instance, produce unlimited amounts of photocopies even if you wish to). More importantly, perhaps, many women teaching Women's Studies do so not from within Women's Studies departments – of which there are still very, very few in Britain – but while based in another discipline, for example English or Social Sciences or Politics.

One of the advantages of Women's Studies is that it can draw on these and other disciplines; its concerns of putting women on to the various cultural and institutional maps, of formulating and utilising ranges of feminist theory and of constructing new women-centred knowledges enable it both to be relevant to all other disciplines and to emerge from these. The latter is what has tended to be the case in Britain; women teaching courses, options or modules on women-centred issues in other subjects have eventually established Women's Studies courses while still operating, and having to operate, in the disciplines in which they started. This can have implications for resourcing, because these days budgets are allocated to cost centres and if you have no visible body (no department, no sizeable course team, etc.) it can mean that the Women's Studies budget will be either a subsection of another department's budget or patched together from various sources, depending on their goodwill rather than on an idea of right. This of course is not invariably the case; some institutions are very supportive of their Women's Studies courses, aware that these courses are highly popular and have no difficulty attracting students.

If tutors on Women's Studies courses are based in other disciplines, they can find themselves short of both time and energy in relation to the Women's Studies course. Having no Women's Studies department often also means having no specific geographical point where students can meet, encounter tutors, find relevant information and so forth. Such lack of material groundedness can make a Women's Studies course quite stressful in that it means the course's existence depends entirely on the bodies of students and tutors present, making them wholly responsible for creating and maintaining the course; they have, in the first instance, to give rather than to take in order to make Women's Studies happen.

Students can find themselves having to deal with resource restraints on time, energy, money, emotion as much as tutors. A Women's Studies course makes demands on you just as much as any other course does; it takes a certain amount of commitment to see it through. If you are faced with competing demands and lack of support concerning course attendance, you have to decide what your priorities are. If you cannot attend fairly regularly, read a certain amount each week and find the time to do assignments, you may need to reconsider the kind of course you are attending – perhaps find one that does not make demands on you which you cannot fulfil. Not being able to participate fully in a course can be very demoralising and ultimately prevent you from completing it.

Another constraint which both staff and students face on Women's Studies courses is that, given its potentially infinite range, there is an overwhelming amount of knowledge from which to choose. It seems that virtually every publisher now brings out at least two 'Women's Studies' or 'Gender Studies' or 'Women's and Gender Studies' catalogues[27] with new publications every year; the sheer quantity of this material makes it impossible for any woman to know more than a very circumscribed area. In other subjects the idea of a specialism is not a problem; in Women's Studies, however, where we are all women (or, at least, mostly so), the fact that we are all women and that the subject is supposed to be about us, that we are supposed to and will have (had) many of the experiences which form the basis for our feminist theories and knowledges, means that there is often an expectation that we should know everything.

I have been to many Women's Studies conferences and meetings where women have bemoaned this very fact, where they have expressed their concern about not being Super-Women's-Studies-woman. How can I speak if I don't know or have not read this or that book; if I have, by chance, not had this or that experience? The implicit (self-)censorship of this stance must be resisted, for it plays into the binarism of expert and novice which has been the basis for the silencing of women. The fact that one cannot know about or contribute to everything should not be a source of anxiety; rather, it is possible to celebrate it as the space in which one can yet discover new things, can learn more. Part of the learning process of Women's Studies is learning that it is not a

subject that can be 'mastered' or 'mistressed', that it is dynamic and can convey that dynamism to its participants. It is a lesson in openness, not in closure.

Problematic Women

When women enter a course they also enter into a contract with those who run the course. It is in this context that women tutors can come to see themselves, and be seen by the students – in Audre Lorde's words cited at the beginning of this chapter – as 'the problematic girls' (or women) hired by the students 'to make them free'. The nature of that contract between students and tutors may be specified in course handbooks, but it actually goes beyond what such handbooks are likely to state – which will not be that tutors have been 'hired to make students free'. But many tutors I have spoken with certainly feel that their role includes attempting to enable and empower students to deal with their situation, whatever that might be. Tutors may feel, in the words of Fiona Norris' 'Classroom Politics':[28]

> They will not forgive us
> These girls
> Sitting in serried rows
> Hungry for attention
> Like shelves of unread books,
> If we do not
> Make the world new for them,
> Teach them to walk
> Into the possibilities
> Of their own becoming,
> Confident in their exploring.

Precisely because Women's Studies addresses and students alike, as women, it often begs precisely the relationship between student or might be.[29] The attempt to establish between students and tutors, derive which stress commonalities and de the question: what is the tutor's Is she or should she be teache mother, lover?

One answer to this ques everything to every woman on

most students would not want that either. In my view, in the first instance tutors are there for students and not the other way round. Second, they are there to enable the students to attempt to do what they came on the course to do, that is to learn about themselves and other women, to develop an understanding of the issues involved in Women's Studies and to acquire relevant skills, possibly to obtain a degree.

Where tutors who teach Women's Studies are also involved in assessing the students, a particularly marked (sic) power relation exists between them, and tutors should be aware of the implications of this. Assessing someone's work is a way of exercising institutionally sanctioned power and has to be seen as such. It puts students and tutors into positions of unequal power.

No one likes everybody whom they encounter to an equal degree; it is therefore very important that tutors are careful about developing 'special' relationships with students whom they particularly like, for whatever reason. Their responsibility is towards every woman on the course. It is not always easy to be equitable. But there is also another, and more pragmatic, factor involved, namely that tutors see new groups of students every year; if they develop 'special' relationships with several students in each new intake, they will quickly suffer from a surfeit of friends. The difficulty is how to do justice to everybody's needs without compromising your own too much, or putting yourself in an impossible situation. For tutors that also means knowing when they cannot help a student further, when that student's specific needs surpass their competence.

Many Women's Studies tutors become very involved in counselling their students and trying to help them deal with their lives. This may seem very altruistic, but it is also associated with the pleasure and satisfaction derived from being regarded as able to 'help' students, being 'wanted', possibly even being made to feel that one is 'in control'. The effect of the reflected glory of students coming to one for advice, which tends to imply that they consider the tutor to be 'together', to know what to do, should not be underestimated. Students' needs can feed tutors' vanities, not necessarily to the advantage of either.

ging Students

dents I have encountered and talked to feel that attending 's Studies course has changed them. Sometimes they over that they do not want or need change; doing the

course then makes them reaffirm the choices they have made in their lives. Sometimes it makes them rethink these choices, both professional and personal ones. Students may be bitten by the 'research' or 'discussion group' bug, and find that they want to carry on doing the kind of work they did for or on the Women's Studies course. Some students decide to change how they act in their professional lives. They can become more assertive and confident in how they argue.

Some students make changes in their personal lives, ask of their partners that they engage with them in different ways, or leave or change their partners. This can be both traumatic and stressful. It is also not specific to Women's Studies but a phenomenon commonly observed among 'mature' students entering courses. Such a student frequently seeks change and will herself change so much during her course attendance that if her partner is not flexible enough to grow with her or accommodate the change, a break is inevitable. This is not the norm, but it can happen. It is also not directly attributable to doing a Women's Studies, or for that matter any other, course. The problems that may lead to the breakup of a relationship are often latently manifest, or even overtly so, before a woman begins a course; doing a course may simply help her to implement changes she has been wanting to make for a while. As Adrienne Rich puts it in 'Prospective Immigrants Please Note':[30]

Either you will
go through this door
or you will not go through.
...
The door itself
makes no promises.
It is only a door.

Notes

1. In Lorde 1982, pp. 49–50 (poem written 1970). Also in: *Undersong*, New York: W.W. Norton.
2. In *The Bloodaxe Book of Contemporary Women Poets*, ed. Jeni Couzyn, Newcastle upon Tyne: Bloodaxe Books, 1985, p. 139.
3. Rich (1980) discusses the need for and possibilities of a university which is gynocentric rather than androcentric.

4. Tania Modleski's *Feminism Without Women*, Marilyn French's *The War Against Women*, and Susan Faludi's *Backlash: The Undeclared War Against Women* all appeared in the early 1990s and all in their different ways testify to this phenomenon (Modleski 1991, French 1992, Faludi 1991).

5. One aspect of this fear is the connection some people make between feminism and lesbianism. For a discussion of this issue in the context of Women's Studies see Frye 1992.

6. Aspen 1983, p. 88.

7. Rich 1978; 1984.

8. An answer to this question is provided by Sandra Coyner (1983). See also France 1983.

9. Texts that may help you to think about this question are Cartledge and Ryan 1983, Jeffreys 1990, McNeill *et al* 1992 or Kitzinger 1985.

10. Textbooks such as Bowles and Duelli Klein 1983 or Jackson *et al* 1993 provide answers to this question.

11. See, for example, Bannerji *et al* 1991.

12. In their recent volume, Sue Wilkinson and Celia Kitzinger (1993) address the issue of feminist women's relationships with men.

13. In Mohin 1979, p. 109.

14. Janice Raymond (1986) discusses diverse only-women communities across a range of cultures.

15. Lorraine Cody (1991) provides some insights into why women are foreign to the academy.

16. See Becher 1989 for a discussion of such territorialities.

17. See, for instance Nkweto Simmonds 1992, Begum 1992, Wilton 1992. All three essays deal with difference in the context of Women's Studies. For a poststructuralist theoretical account see, for example, Butler and Scott 1992.

18. Peggy Phelan (1993) deals in an interesting way with the issue of visibility and identity politics.

19. Perhaps the best-known writer on racism and feminism is bell hooks whose books of 1982, 1984 and 1989 all deal with this issue. I also recommend Trinh T. Minh-Ha 1989.

20. See Wilton 1993, or the sections entitled 'Lesbians in the Academic World: The Personal/Political Experience' and 'In the Classroom', both in Cruikshank 1982, for further discussions of this issue.

21. See Matthews and Thompson 1993 for a further view on this issue.

22. Breeze 1992, p. 74.

23. Rich 1981, pp. 21–2; 1984.
24. In Mohin 1979, p. 112.
25. An interesting novel by Gillian Hanscombe (1983) fiction-alises and explores this issue.
26. Delphi and Leonard 1992 is pertinent here.
27. The inverted commas and variety of titles indicate a current issue about the 'nature' of Women's Studies, reflected in publishers' changeable targeting of audiences in their publicity. 'Women's Studies' is women-centred; 'Gender Studies' – neutral though the phrase is supposed to seem – introduces masculinity as a significant topic. I have come across one case of a course entitled 'Women's and Gender Studies', where the first half obviously catered for women while the second half was the men's playing field. Routledge's 1993/4 'Gender and Women's Studies' catalogue features on its cover two nearly nude men in posing pouches, one on a pedestal, the other adoringly kneeling at the foot of the pedestal rapturously gazing up. Women are nowhere to be seen, and as much as that image may function as an ironic commentary (but perhaps that's rather a hopeful reading?), it begs the questions: 'Where are the women?' and 'Is this what women want?'
28. In Raving Beauties 1985, p. 119.
29. It is easy to avoid thinking about this relationship despite the fact that, at least in my experience, Women's Studies tutors certainly discuss it among themselves quite a lot. Noreen O'Connor and Joanna Ryan (1993) offer a relevant parallel discussion on women therapists and their clients in the context of lesbianism and psychoanalysis.
30. Rich 1984.

References and Further Reading

Aspen (1983), 'For My "Apolitical" Sisters', in Raving Beauties, eds, *In the Pink* (London: Women's Press), p. 88.

Bannerji, H., L. Carty, K. Delhi, S. Heald and K. McKenna, eds (1991), *Unsettling Relations: The University as a Site of Feminist Struggles* (Boston, MA: South End).

Becher, T. (1989), *Academic Tribes and Territories: Intellectual Enquiry and the Cultures of Disciplines* (Guildford: SRHE).

Begum, N. (1992), 'Disabled Women and the Feminist Agenda' in H. Hinds, A. Phoenix and J. Stacey, eds, *Working Out: New Directions for Women's Studies* (London: Falmer), pp. 61–73.

Bowles, G. and R. Duelli Klein, eds (1983), *Theories of Women's Studies* (London: Routledge).

Breeze, J.B. (1992), *Spring Cleaning* (London: Virago).

Butler, J. and J.W. Scott, eds (1992), *Feminists Theorize the Political* (London: Routledge).

Cartledge, S. and J. Ryan, eds (1983), *Sex & Love: New Thoughts on Old Contradictions* (London: Women's Press).

Coyner, S. (1983),'Women's Studies as an Academic Discipline: Why and How to Do It' in G. Bowles and R. Duelli Klein, eds, *Theories of Women's Studies* (London: Routledge), pp. 46–71.

Cruikshank, M., ed. (1982), *Lesbian Studies: Present and Future* (New York: Feminist Press).

Delphi, C. and D. Leonard (1992), *Familiar Exploitations: A New Analysis of Marriage in Contemporary Western Societies* (Cambridge: Polity).

Faludi, S. (1991), *Backlash: The Undeclared War against Women* (London: Chatto & Windus).

Feldman, S.D. (1974), *Escape from the Doll's House* (New York: McGraw-Hill).

France, M. (1983), 'Why Women's Studies?', in *Women's Studies International Forum*, vol. 6, no. 3, pp. 305–8.

French, M. (1992), *The War against Women* (London: Hamish Hamilton).

Frye, M. (1992), 'Willful Virgin or Do You Have to Be a Lesbian to Be a Feminist?', in *Willful Virgin: Essays in Feminism* (Freedom, CA: Crossing Press), pp. 124–37.

Fulton, O. (1989), *Access and Institutional Change* (Guildford: SRHE).

Hanscombe, G. (1983), *Between Friends* (London: Sheba Feminist Publishers).

Hevner Mueller, K. (1954), *Educating Women for a Changing World* (University of Minnesota Press).

hooks, bell (1982), *Ain't I a Woman: Black Women and Feminism* (London: Pluto).

—— (1984), *Feminist Theory: From Margin to Centre* (Boston, MA: South End).

—— (1989), *Talking Back: Thinking Feminist – Thinking Black* (London: Sheba Feminist Publishers).

Jackson, S. *et al* eds (1993), *Women's Studies: A Reader* (Hemel Hempstead: Harvester Wheatsheaf).

Jeffreys, S. (1990), *Anticlimax: A Feminist Perspective on the Sexual Revolution* (London: Women's Press).

Kitzinger, S. (1985), *Woman's Experience of Sex* (London: Penguin).

Lorde, A. (1982), *Chosen Poems – Old and New* (London: W.W. Norton & Co).

Matthews, J. and L. Thompson (1993), 'Disability as a Focus for Innovation in Women's Studies and Access Strategies in Higher Education', in M. Kennedy, C. Lubelska and V. Walsh, eds, *Making Connections: Women's Studies, Women's Movements, Women's Lives* (London: Falmer), pp. 130–44.

McNeill, P., B. Freeman and J. Newman, eds (1992), *Women Talk Sex* (London: Scarlet).

Minh-Ha, T. (1989), *Woman Native Other* (Bloomington: University of Indiana Press).

Modleski, T. (1991), *Feminism without Women* (London: Routledge).

Mohin, L., ed. (1979), *One Foot on the Mountain* (London: Onlywomen).

Nkweto Simmonds, F. (1992), 'Difference, Power and Knowledge: Black Women in Academia' in H. Hinds, A. Phoenix and J. Stacey, eds. *Working Out: New Directions for Women's Studies* (London: Falmer), pp. 51–60.

O'Connor, N. and J. Ryan (1993), *Wild Desires and Mistaken Identities: Lesbianism and Psychoanalysis* (London: Virago).

Phelan, P. (1993), *Unmarked: The Politics of Performance* (London: Routledge).

Raving Beauties (1983), *In the Pink* (London: Women's Press).

——, eds (1985), *No Holds Barred* (London: Women's Press).

Rich, A. (1978), 'Cartographies of Silence', in *The Dream of a Common Language* (London: W.W. Norton & Co), pp. 16–20.

—— (1980), 'Toward a Woman-Centered University' in *On Lies, Secrets, Silence: Selected Prose 1966–1978* (London: Virago), pp. 125–56.

—— (1981), *A Wild Patience Has Taken Me This Far* (W.W. Norton & Co).

—— (1984), 'Prospective Immigrants Please Note', in *The Fact of a Doorframe* (London: W.W. Norton & Co), pp. 51–2.

—— (1991), *An Atlas of the Difficult World: Poems 1988-1991* (London: W.W. Norton & Co).

Wilkinson, S. and C. Kitzinger, eds (1993), *Heterosexuality: A 'Feminism & Psychology' Reader* (London: Sage).

Wilton, T. (1992), 'Desire and the Politics of Representation: Issues for Lesbians and Heterosexual Women' in H. Hinds, A. Phoenix and J. Stacey, eds, *Working Out: New Directions for Women's Studies* (London: Falmer), pp. 74–85.

—— (1993), 'Queer Subjects: Lesbians, Heterosexual Women and the Academy', in M. Kennedy, C. Lubelska and V. Walsh, eds, *Making Connections: Women's Studies, Women's Movements, Women's Lives* (London: Falmer), pp. 167–79.

Section II

Women's Studies Students

2

Deborah: The Validation of My Black Self

Coming out of a situation where she had not been encouraged to think of herself as academically capable, Deborah, a divorced mother of two, decided to re-enter education in her 30s. Attending Women's Studies courses, especially one with a focus on the Caribbean, enabled her to build up confidence in her self as a Black, intellectually competent woman and to take pride in her background.

Making Decisions

I'm 36 years old. I came on the Women's Studies course because other subjects like Maths, Science, Sociology and Psychology were so focused on men and I wanted to hear things more from a woman's point of view. With other subjects you couldn't get involved personally in the same way. When I saw the information about Women's Studies I thought, yes, this is right for me because I can give MY interpretation of how I see things as well as hear other women's views.

I've got two children and am going through a divorce which is very traumatic, so it's very hard at the moment. The breakup of my marriage started around the time I got on the course. After the initial shock of my husband going, and getting him to file for divorce, I thought, 'How do I cope?' In my mind I had all these negative stereotyped images of women whose husbands leave and the women then break down, they can't cope and they can't do anything because they depended on this man so much, not realising that it was they who were strong, who kept the house going and kept the marriage and the family together.

I worked throughout my marriage, I worked right through my pregnancies and after the children were born, and I was strong. But I didn't see that I was strong within the marriage because I suppress a lot. In relationships, I suppress so much of myself to keep this man on a pedestal, to keep the patriarchal system, his macho image going, to pacify him and to play down my own position. You lose things within yourself. It was only after him going and millions of tears later that I thought, 'No, I've got to continue, I've got my children to bring up.' That was what made me continue to grow and to be strong. I don't know if I didn't have my children how long it would have taken me to get over him.

I decided to go back into education because I didn't do well at school. I finished school the earliest time possible, which was about 15 and a half, because no one was pushing me. I suffered from asthma as a child anyway, so I missed a lot of schooling and found it hard to catch up. I was constantly being told that I was stupid and that I was not going to be very academic but I'd be a good wife. I was always told to do things IN THE HOUSE but reading books was not for me. It was my older sister Palorine who was the reader and who did really well, getting degrees. I'm really proud of her.

It was after I had my last child that I got really fed up at work, because I wasn't going anywhere, it wasn't giving me any status. I was a medical receptionist, which is a job in which there is no possibility of promotion. Although the work was lovely because you could get involved with the patients and the doctors, I wasn't going up on any ladder. Also, I needed to get more money, which you can't get without promotion, and I thought that I'd either have to get another job or get back into education.

I did an Access course which I found bloody hard because I had been out of education for over 15 years and I hadn't been the best of students at school anyway. All that came rushing back in flashbacks, making me think, 'I don't know what I'm doing here because I'm not that clever, I'm not that smart.' Being called 'stupid' and 'thick' and 'unintelligent' had lasted all through my life; even now, although I have achieved and am achieving, it is still there and I still ask myself, 'Am I really doing this?', 'Is this really me?'

Doing the Access course helped me overcome the difficulty of thinking, 'Can I do this?' It didn't particularly help me in relation to my current course because some of the things we were taught were no use. We didn't even have an exam at the end of the Access course; having exams now is a bit of a shock. But for all that, the Access course gave me a lift back into education; without it I probably wouldn't be doing a degree now.

Validating My Caribbean Identity

Getting on the Women's Studies course, for me, was like a dream. When I got accepted I came out crying and my sister asked, 'Why

are you crying so? What made you think you wouldn't get on?'
I couldn't wait to start. It was really an excitement and a very
positive excitement.

Although the course is very hard to do, I just love it, love it in
the respect that I am getting to know writers like Simone de
Beauvoir and Dale Spender, who I didn't know much about
before. I am getting to know their names, though I haven't read
their books in depth because I mainly read a lot of Black books
by writers like Alice Walker, bell hooks, Maya Angelou and Merle
Collins, because I want to get my own identity into a Black
perspective first, before I get to grips with a white perspective. White
women talk but they don't really know me, they don't really know
us.

I am also doing a Caribbean Studies unit which offers a Women's
Studies section. This course is run by Merle Collins, who is a lecturer
and a well-known writer. At the moment we are looking at women
in the Caribbean and the family and kinship systems. That unit
relates more to me than the other Women's Studies course because
I can get to grips with being Caribbean, which is important to
me because I'm a Caribbean woman, though I left there when I
was five and don't know much about it. The language used in the
Caribbean, for example, is completely different from the language
used here, but it is still incorporated on the course, which is
really good.

But I also really enjoy the non-Caribbean Women's Studies
course; I'm lucky because I get a balance between the two: I can
understand the Caribbean side AND the European, the English
side of Women's Studies, which is great.

Looking at women in the Caribbean is helping me understand
my own and my family's situation. I've got both my mother and
my grandmother here, and their behaviours are quite different.
My mother, for example, has her West Indian side but she tries
to be English, to fit into English ways, though she doesn't need
to. But because she has worked in this country she has felt that
she needed to try and fit in. We begin to lose our self when we
come to another country – you take on that country's way of life
and attitudes and you lose your own. You may keep it within
yourself, your own family, but you lose it when you go out and
you try to talk 'like them', act like them, be like them, adopt their
behaviour. You do all that and try to fit in but still they don't bloody
want you to be like them. My grandmother, who never worked
in this country, doesn't have any of these inhibitions and desires
to be like British people. She talks how she talks, she cusses – you

say 'swear', we say 'cuss' – she cusses. These sorts of differences among Caribbean women which occur when they leave the islands are discussed on the Caribbean course, things like how you sit in the kitchen and listen to your grandmother telling you about home, how it was when they were young, and how they see the children of today. They see today's children as not having any manners or respect for the older people, especially those in England. Then somebody else on the course will come in and tell you about their grandmother, saying, 'My Gran does that,' or, 'My Mum does that,' and your heart just swells because it's so 'real', it's not just textbooks speaking. Even when the material is from textbooks, it still relates to YOU, which is wonderful.

For me, doing the Caribbean unit is validating my identity. I didn't know much about the Caribbean and I was well impressed that there are a lot of Caribbean writers, Caribbean movements and groups. The Caribbean has always had political movements, which I didn't know about. I didn't even realise that in St Vincent, where I come from, there was a woman in the 1930s called Elma François who started a Women's Movement. That was astonishing for me. On a small island like that they had movements, they had organisations and unions – I thought that sort of thing only existed in England and in America.

Black women in Britain aren't usually encouraged to look at their own country or island as significant or doing anything significant – doing the Caribbean unit has enabled me to say, 'I'm proud to be a Caribbean woman, to be Black and to come from St Vincent.' When I was at school, I never told people that I was from the Caribbean, that I was from St Vincent, because they'd say, 'Where's that?' That made me think that it couldn't be an important place, so I used to say I was from Jamaica. People know of Jamaica because it's a bigger island, so I used to pretend I was from there. I look back now, thinking, 'Jesus, I totally denied my own culture, my island, so I could fit in with somebody else's expectation that I must be Jamaican or African.' I can now feel proud because St Vincent figures on the course and there are women out there who made a stand and were involved in movements and I can read about them. I can now interpret negative attitudes to my own children and offer them positive images of St Vincent and the rest of the Caribbean, and say, 'OK, you're British because of where you were born, but you have a Caribbean past and you can draw on that. That's something to be proud of.'

On the Caribbean unit are not only Black Caribbean women but also white women. There's even a Black Caribbean man. He's a percentage of nothing. He doesn't give us negative feedback – well, he can't. The course isn't just 'us', a Black women's ghetto, but it is also nice that it has a majority of Black women, which is good for me because in every other course or unit I am in the minority. Being part of the majority is wonderful because you have more control.

Self-Empowerment through Education

Education is the most respected thing in the Caribbean. Women, even in rural areas, know that it is education that's going to get them out of their poverty. Women are encouraged to take up education, to become nurses and teachers. Education is treated very differently in the Caribbean to here. Over there you HAVE to go. If you play truant you get a beating. There's a lot of pressure to go. If people get found out they get a proper telling off from the parents AND from the teacher. Neighbours will tell your parents if they see you in the street when you should be at school. Nobody here takes any notice of kids bunking off or asks them, 'Why aren't you at school?' Discipline is much greater in the Caribbean than here – over there you're shit scared of the teacher. Nobody would rape or beat up a teacher like some students do here.

I left school very early. I was constantly told that I was no good at school but that I would be a good wife because I could cook and clean and tidy really well and look after children. I completely internalised what I was told and just accepted that I wasn't supposed to be any good at school. Even when I went to work and did secretarial jobs, typing and all that, I didn't praise myself for that. Nothing positive for me came out of me. I feel positive NOW that I have achieved bringing up my children on my own, coping with life's problems in general, as well as getting on the course – all that is only now coming out, in my later life. Before I had no encouragement, I was very negative and I didn't think anything of myself.

The Women's Studies course gave me hope because being about WOMEN it made me think that I would be able to cope with the subject more easily than, say, straight English or Maths or Sociology, and that I'd do better this time round with my education. The fact that the subject is about women, is taught by women and has a majority of women students made it seem more related to myself and my experiences. All I could think about was getting on the course and enjoying it. I had no particular long-term expectations of what I wanted to do at the end of the course.

The first few sessions on the course were terribly exciting. I was on a high, being in a class with all these women and thinking, 'I don't have to compete with men here.' If you're in a class with boys or men, you end up either competing with them or flirting with them. This, I felt, was much better. I didn't have to compete and I didn't have to flirt. I could just get on with my work and I could relate to somebody else, another woman. I could go to her and ask her how to do something without having to go to a man and wondering whether, in exchange for help with my work, I'd have to go to a pub with him or something.

One of the frustrating aspects of the subject is that whatever is described as women's fate in the past still seems to be women's fate now. It makes me wonder when things are going to change for women. It seems to take years and years for anything to change. If you look at women's history in the Army or women's involvement in technology, you realise that women have never got recognition or acknowledgements for their contributions and this is still going on now. It's taken so long for anything to improve, especially in Black women's lives. Attitudes within institutions such as education and in the workplace still have to change a lot. Education itself needs to contribute more to encouraging change, and women themselves have to change, they have to stop giving in to men, and to the pressure to conform with traditional roles and values.

One of the best things about the Women's Studies course for me is being seen as someone who IS capable of doing academic work. I used to be the one who got the lowest marks at school; now, being able to hand in assignments and get good grades is amazing and enabling for me. It gives me the strength and spirit to go on.

I haven't got a very clear idea of what I want to do afterwards. I'm toying with the idea of doing a postgraduate degree because I love learning now, I love education. At school I never liked it because I didn't understand what was going on. I didn't feel able to raise my hand and ask questions when I didn't understand something – now I do, I can understand the value of education and I want my own children to know and understand that value.

3

Peggy: Feminist Leanings

Peggy moved from Canada to Britain in the 1970s. A history of feeling disadvantaged because she is a woman, a fear of achieving which had meant starting and stopping many different things, combined with her career as a housewife and mother, led her to do an MA in Women's Studies when she was 40.

'Feminist Leanings'

I started the MA in Women's Studies when I was 40 years old. I hadn't been looking to do a course but I'd just been turned down as a magistrate and I figured that if I couldn't be a magistrate I'd do a Masters degree instead. I was due to be sworn in as a magistrate, but then I got a speeding ticket, and about seven days before I was due for the swearing in I had a letter which I had to sign to say that I had no convictions, so I had to declare the speeding ticket and they wrote back, saying thank you for your interest but we do not require your services after all.

I had been doing a counselling course and several courses with the Open University on cognitive psychology and so on prior to coming on the MA. A very good friend of mine was doing a Combined Studies degree at the local college; she came one day and said, 'I've seen something you'll love, an MA in Women's Studies.' My friend thought I would like the course because she knew I had feminist leanings. She knew that I felt there was a terrible inequality in the system which I couldn't really articulate then, put it into words even if I'd tried. I thought, 'There's no way I'm going to get on an MA – I haven't got a first degree.' But my friend said that they'd take people with no first degrees, so I rang up and asked about it. Then I went to see a tutor on the course who made me feel very confident about attending the course, saying, 'You're just the sort of person we're looking for.' But when I got invited for a proper interview I was immediately completely crestfallen and thought I wouldn't be able to come on the course.

As far as my 'feminist leanings' were concerned, I didn't, in a sense, even know how to spell the word feminist at the time when

I entered the course. When I was asked at the interview if I was a feminist, I said, 'I think so – but I'm not a man-hater,' and the tutor said, 'No, nor am I, and I am married,' and so on, and I was quite relieved to hear that because at that time my 'feminist leanings' went strictly by the Oxford Dictionary definition that I advocated rights for women while not denying rights for men. So they were about equality and fairness, which is really important to me though I realise that it doesn't exist.

Contradictions around Women and Attainment

That's because I have been subject to unfairness all my life – constantly. For instance, I was very much a second-class citizen in my own family although there were three girls and four boys. The girls were always second-class citizens. My parents' hopes and aspirations were very divided. My mother wanted me to do big things with my life because she never had. My father really wanted to marry off his daughters and get them out of the house. On every level – social, academic, sporting, with regard to sex particularly – there was a complete double standard in my home. At high school most of my friends were very academic and came from very fair backgrounds where their parents encouraged them as much as the sons to pursue academe if that's the way they were inclined. In my case I know that it was expected that girls became nurses, stewardesses or teachers and then they got married. None of those things appealed to me.

My family was not stereotypical for Canada. I think they were a confused mess of repressed feelings, my father coming from a Presbyterian background. It was all right to drink alcohol for medicinal purposes and a lot of people drank a lot of alcohol for that purpose. Women didn't drink. While my father came from that sort of repressed background, my mother came from a very aristocratic English background and was a terrible snob, but she also realised in her later years that education is the only way out of the rut that she had found herself in. She didn't want me to make the same mistakes she had made.

Given the contradictions around women and attainment in my family, I think I went to university because it was expected of me. My choice was a very immature choice, made mostly by my mother. She said to me at one point in my life, 'I live through you' – and she did. She lived vicariously through me, academically, socially. All the things that I did my mother wanted to do. When I did a parachute jump I can remember her saying, 'Oh, I've always wanted to do that but only you have got the courage.' There was an enormous pressure on me to succeed for my mother as well as for myself.

I think that's probably why I failed – because I was doing things for her rather than for myself. I didn't want to do physiotherapy, I didn't want to do rehabilitative medicine at university. I didn't feel I was qualified for it, I didn't feel it was what my mother thought it was, and I did it because she wanted me to. That was the biggest pressure that was ever put on me, to be something for her, and I was also seen by my brothers and sisters as the favourite, the talented kid in the family. I swam in competitions, I did diving, gymnastics; academically I wasn't a great achiever in my view but I could do just about anything I turned my hand to. But as soon as I got good at something, I quit because I was so frightened of the responsibility of carrying that.

I didn't really have a sense of what I wanted to do and even now I am still wondering what I want to be when I grow up. I know I'm nearly 43, but I still feel enormous pressure to be things other than what I want to be. I think I'm getting closer to knowing what I want to do with my life other than being a mother, other than being a wife. But I must be really slow to mature, because I've never really known what I wanted.

For the Rest of My Life?

Moving from Canada to England affected me very badly. I hadn't really thought about it in any depth much until one of my tutors on the Women's Studies course raised it as a question, suggesting that I might have left Canada so that I could carry on with my anorexic behaviours in the relative privacy of a quiet marital home. I think there was some truth in that because I did a lot of travelling, and whenever I did that it was really to escape the decision of what I was going to do with the rest of my life.

I came to England through meeting my husband in Vancouver. He came to be best man at the wedding of a friend of mine who was working at the newspaper where I worked between terms at university. It was like another of these 'match-made-in-heaven' crap stories where a friend would come and say, 'I've got a man for you, Peggy. You're going to love this guy,' and then I'd meet these revolting creeps. So I said to him that I was not going to go out any more with any of his horrible friends from England but he said, 'No, this one's different.' And he was.

I met my husband, wrote to him throughout the following year, then came over in the following spring and was married almost immediately after. I didn't know him at all. I'd only been out with him twice when we married. The fact that I didn't know him at all when I married him suggests to me now that I was trying to escape from Vancouver.

In some respects I relived what I had had at home but under better, ideal conditions. The expectations he had of me were also rather similar to those of my mother. He encouraged me in every way to do what I wanted to do with my life as long as I didn't flap my wings too hard. As soon as I showed any form of independence or being able to cope on my own, he called a halt to what I was doing. For example: I had a teaching post and was offered the head of department position, and he said that he'd got a promotion and we had to move. There was no question in his mind that I would stay and take on the job. We were moving. His promotion took precedent over mine. At the time I did not even consider questioning it. I immediately handed in my resignation and we moved. I don't remember ever thinking, 'No, we must stay.' I can feel bitter about it, but in reality I think I was frightened of the responsibility so it was convenient that it happened.

Convenient Accidents?

I was 21 when I married and had my first child when I was 27 or 28. In between I worked as a teacher for a while. I did a graphic design course. I started a lot of things and finished very few. With the graphic design course, I was just coming to the end of it and to my final exams when my mother's cancer recurred. I always had these sort of timely things take place that were tragedies in the background, that always stopped me from achieving my own – like my husband being promoted, and suddenly I couldn't be the head of department. That sort of thing always seemed to come along.

But in retrospect I see them as rather convenient accidents because they stopped me achieving anything. I was frightened of achieving anything because then I might actually have to go out and get a job. I've always been terrified of independence, real independence, and I still dream of being turned out of the house without a job as a teenager, with no husband to take care of me, with nothing. I have an incredible fear that I can't support myself. I think that was indoctrinated into me, that I couldn't do it on my own, that I needed a man to take care of me, that I needed to marry. That was probably why it was my goal to find a man who could support me and take care of me, and then I could relax and didn't have to be independent. When I did find the man who could do that I didn't relax, I just pursued my anorexia with a vengeance, I suspect because of the conflict in my childhood all the time to achieve on the one hand for my mother.

Matters of Confidence

The idea I got of the Women's Studies course was that it was very historical and I thought I wasn't going to like that. Then I was intimidated even more at the interview by being handed a list of books by authors I had never ever read. I am pleased now because I know these writers. When Toni Morrison won the Nobel Prize for Literature, I thought, I've read three of her books. And when people talk about Virginia Woolf now, I don't just think of Liz Taylor and *Who's Afraid of Virgina Woolf?* any more. So I'm pleased that I did the course, but at the beginning I was intimidated because I thought all the people teaching Women's Studies are high up in the academic hierarchy. And of course all the tutors were doctors. So I felt quite threatened by that. As regards other students, when I first came on the course I was overwhelmed by the people on it. My initial reaction was that they were just what I'd thought they'd be, they're all a bunch of academics, and then I realised that some of them were no more academic than me, and I also realised that I was perhaps a little bit more academic than I thought I was.

But I thought that if I kept my head down I could probably bullshit my way through it, as I had done with most things. Most of the courses I had taken until this MA were a combination of a smattering of knowledge and a lot of bullshit. Counselling in particular. The more feelings you could write on a piece of paper, the more counselling people love it. I still see myself as academically inadequate and when people ask me what I've written in my MA dissertation, I tend to say, 'Oh, just a lot of bullshit.'

I think I'm only just beginning, as a result of doing the MA, to believe in myself. Sometimes I open my thesis and read a bit to myself and think that if I could write what it says in there, I must have understood something of the subject. I'm just beginning to think of myself as someone who has a bit of knowledge. But I always emphasise that it's only a little. I have been through a pretence for most of my life, believing that people see me as something I am not. They see me as quite intelligent, as quite assertive and reasonably confident. But that belies what's actually going on inside me. The best thing about the MA was that when I demonstrated inadequacy I didn't have a whole lot of people turn on me and look at me as if I was an idiot. In fact, I was congratulated, with people saying, 'I'm glad you asked that.' I remember once asking, 'What does "genre" mean?' and rather than being made to look a fool, the tutor simply explained what it meant, and afterwards I was congratulated by various other students on the course who all said they didn't know what it meant. Then it became a joke in our group and I remember once using the word 'vignette' and when asked what it meant, saying 'salad dressing', and suddenly it became acceptable not to know what a word meant. I think there was a huge fear around that for a while. So then you become the person who has the courage to ask the question. So things actually reversed themselves for me, and it was the first time in my life that I had the courage, but probably the safety, to say what was up.

I had a very grey idea of what feminism was at that point. It wasn't really until we began to explore the different facets of feminism and I began to read *Feminist Thought* and several other books that I realised that Jean Plaidy was not a historian after all. Then people began to discuss it, began to discuss their ideas outside the classroom as well. If you took the package of all the people I met on this course, you would have a smattering of just about every kind of feminism that exists, and some that have never been given labels. I would also say that there are some who could not by any stretch of the imagination call themselves feminists. Myself, I still adhere to the original definition of advocating rights for women, because I'm not sure where I stand with regard to feminism. I've learnt so much about feminism in the last two years that, if anything, it's confused me rather than clarified where I stand. I know I have stronger views – because I'm able to articulate them better – on everything, from basics such as equality between the sexes to the way in which patriarchy infiltrates everything that we do.

My views are changing all the time, they're very liquid. I'd always felt there was a huge injustice. I think from a very simplistic point of view, I could look at my husband and say, 'I am as capable and as intelligent as my husband, but there's no way I could go out and pull his salary, no matter how much training, no matter how many qualifications I have.' Some of that has to do with the fact that I cannot interact with people the way my husband can, but a lot of it has to do with the fact that I am a female. I am realising a lot of things now. Before, I'd emphasise that it's my being a female which meant I couldn't pull in that salary. I realise now that it isn't just that. It's my actually attempting to do it, to go out and attempt to work my way up as my husband has, and I realise that I was stopped or I stopped myself from doing that for years, one because I felt I had no right, and two because I didn't think I had the ability. I didn't really believe in myself at all. That has changed to some extent.

I don't have great confidence now. But for the first time in my life, I feel that I have a contribution to make other than through helping people. One of the reasons I decided not to do charitable work any more was that I want to put a value, a monetary value, on what I do. And there's no reason why I shouldn't, although I never felt justified in doing that before because I have a husband who earns a fantastic salary so I have no justification in going out and earning money. That wasn't really what I meant though; what I meant was I am *not entitled* to earn money because I have no qualifications. Now I see that differently.

The Course Experience

The MA in Women's Studies was wonderful. I have nothing but positive feelings about it. That is strange because when I look back on other courses that I've done, there were times when I'd have happily dropped them right in the middle, and I soldiered on because I developed a huge sense of purpose that I must finish things that I started – that was so for my counselling course, for example. But with the MA in Women's Studies, I didn't want it to end. I wanted to get the thesis out of the way but I wanted the course to carry on because, like so many people on the course, I felt that we had only just scratched the surface, and I felt the real work, the real investigation, the real exploring came after the dissertation when you could look at all the things you hadn't done yet. The course was probably one of the best experiences I've had; certainly from an academic viewpoint, it was the very best experience – for my own self-esteem, if nothing else. I remember particularly people sharing; one tutor once talked about her marriage and said that if she had the choice she probably wouldn't do it again but still live with her husband, and I remember thinking at the time that that sort of candidness could only exist on a Women's Studies course. I think everyone thought that.

I enjoyed the early stages of the course in particular, of being told to read a particular book and coming back and discussing it, and hearing everyone else's views and perceptions of what that book was about. I liked the structuredness of some of the sessions, the classroom format, because it was something that I could relate to. It also fed me information which I needed because my ideas about many things weren't very clear; I was just like a sponge waiting to soak up all this information. That's why I liked some of the structuredness of it. Before attending the course I had never, for example, thought about gynaecology and medicine and how androcentric it was, but when we sat down, and looked at its history and women's personal stories came out, the humiliation, the degradation, the subjugation – everything that all of us had experienced, including the most confident and assertive women on the course who all had been victimised by patriarchal medicine ... I never thought that everyone had had that experience.

Because I'm a gregarious person I loved the study group time, but we never used that time productively. We used to sit talking, exchanging information, just chat. They were a social time, a lovely time, and I wouldn't take them out. Perhaps they should be called 'happy hour'.

My relationship with people on the course changed dramatically over time. I, and I think a lot of people felt that way, started out feeling, 'God, I've got a naff lot here – I could have been put into a more interesting group,' but by the end I felt I'd been given the *crème de la crème*. I wasn't terribly happy in the beginning, thinking I wouldn't like the group; looking around the room there were other people I would have been more obviously interested in and I didn't seem to have any of them in my group. But then I realised I had all of them. When I took my time and got to know them, I realised I was wrong. What made my group good was that we had the most diverse of all the groups. In some study groups there were all teachers or all social workers. But we had everything in our group, from a woman who was in a very high-powered position at work and who had sufficient self-esteem not to need to project herself on to anyone, to a woman who, although she had achieved an awful lot in a man's trade, had just about no self-esteem at all. Some were feminist, one very definitely wasn't.

I was only a housewife, which I found quite difficult. When the MA in Women's Studies first started people got up and said things like, 'I am doing Women's Studies because ...' and it reminded me of the sort of cocktail hour when everyone says, 'I am doing a counselling course because I am a personnel director at ICI,' and I felt terribly inadequate that I was a housewife. It's a label that's dumped on women when they've got nothing else to put on a form. And somehow I always wanted to be able to say, 'student/housewife' or 'doctor/housewife', something important/housewife. Society as a whole devalues housework, and I find it hard to value it myself. I still think, 'When am I going to go out and do a real job?' So I think I still devalue what I do, though maybe not as much as I did when I started the course.

The initial effect of the course was that I began to read far more broadly than I'd ever done before, and I don't just pick books up at the Tesco book-selection shelf any more. I believe in myself more. When I want to and when I'm ready to, I will be able to do what I want to do. And I feel I made some good friends on the course too, people that I think I could call up and feel at ease with, despite the fact that I'm a housewife. I've become more critical, more critical of society as a whole, more critical of women for colluding in patriarchy, for being party to so much that's wrong, for indoctrinating their children in the same inequalities that we have undergone. I have made actual changes in my life, particularly with my husband. A lot of things have changed in our domestic life, and a lot of things have changed in how we bring our children up. My daughter is not a second-class citizen as I felt I was; to me she never has been. But I allowed my husband for years to have a bonding with his son that he didn't have with our daughter. And I won't allow now for her to be excluded from things, or for her to be tagged on, 'Oh, and you can come and watch,' which I suffered from a lot in the early years of my marriage, where it was, 'You can come and make the tea while the men play rugby,' that sort of thing. Not that I wanted to go and play rugby, but I was damned if I was going to go and stand on the sidelines. And I don't want my daughter to experience that. So our domestic life has changed. And my attitude towards work has changed – I have stopped doing voluntary work now.

I have become more feminist, and I've noticed that when I discuss things with my husband this comes out as a derogatory term as well: 'As a feminist, *you would* think that.' This is an issue for me because I would like to think that my husband is a feminist as well, but when it comes to the crunch, backs against the wall, I think men are threatened by feminism. It threatens their position. My feminism threatens my husband. But I don't see it as threatening in a bad way. I see it as threatening in ways that open up all kinds of new venues for him. For instance, he is getting to know our daughter better. I don't want to suggest that he hasn't been a good father to her before, but his fatherhood now doesn't necessarily stop at his maleness. He has, for example, on occasions said to me, 'Well, you should talk to her about that,' and I think, 'Why?', 'Why should I talk to her about AIDS or condoms – why shouldn't you?' ,'Why should it come from a woman?' I think my husband can see the benefits of that but is threatened by it sometimes.

4

Suki: Dealing with Sexism

Suki, a mixed-race woman with a history of modelling and doing a Business Studies course, came to Women's Studies through a fluke and found that it provided her with a basis for examining, through making a tape-slide, her relationship with her father, as well as enabling her to analyse the various kinds of sexism she'd come across in her life.

Coming to Women's Studies

I am 31 now. I had a gap of ten years out of education before I went on an HND Business Studies course. I did my 'A' levels, but at that time I was not really interested in continuing my studies. Immediately after my 'A' levels I took a year out, then I got into modelling and the one year stretched into ten. I didn't take the year out to model – it happened after I'd made a decision not to continue with my education immediately.

I'm not very proud of having been a model. I have strong feelings about the negative representations of women in popular culture, and I think the fashion industry and models do *not* provide positive role models for young women, as well as putting enormous pressure on women to conform to stereotyped images. Anna Ford's 'body fascism', that sort of thing. I wasn't happy being part of that. Also, there's a lot of money in the fashion business and it seemed somehow obscene to me, the amounts that got wasted. It wasn't very easy and I have very mixed feelings about that whole time. I had an opportunity to travel and I did a lot of things – that was positive for me.

Then I came to a grinding halt with all of that and didn't really know what to do with myself. I decided that maybe it was time to get back into education. I chose to do a vocational course, thinking it would help me with my future. The course I got on had a good reputation and was close to where I was living at the time. Then, as I was studying, I decided that I wanted to do a degree course rather than an HND course which is what I was doing at the time. I began to enjoy studying and started to think about going on to another course. There were grant considerations and

I wanted to stay reasonably close to the area I am in. In the end, East London offered me the opportunity I was looking for.

When I applied for courses, I didn't realise Women's Studies courses were available, but when I went to the institution I am at now on one of the preview days I found out about the course. The Women's Studies course sounded really interesting and the possibility of a 'Women and Technology' course seemed to fit in with my Business Studies course; it all sounded great, so I ended up doing Women's Studies instead of Psychology, which was what I had intended to do. I did only two business units in the end – the rest were all Women's Studies ones.

Apart from the usual 'Women's Studies – what is it?' questions, most people thought doing Women's Studies was something of a change in direction for me and might in fact be a bit too much of a change in direction, that it would go against me when I came to apply for jobs. But I had it all worked out in my head by this time; on the Business Studies course I'd been bothered by the tokenism of women's issues. To me it seemed like a natural way of balancing out the biases I had been exposed to on my previous course.

The Difference of Women's Studies

When I first started everything seemed to be a bit disjointed; being a Combined Studies student of which Women's Studies was only a part was quite tricky. Doing Women's Studies was a big change from my previous course; the methods of teaching as such weren't very different, but the attitudes of the lecturers to the students and the whole atmosphere of the actual classroom situation, the contact were very different. In a lot of respects, it was the other side of the coin to my previous course. In the 'Women and Technology' unit, we were told all the things that had been left out of the Business Studies course. There we had one lecturer whose work I subsequently used on the Women's Studies course; she was described as a bit of a radical feminist on the HND course and she was treated – certainly by the other students – as if she was a complete loony, a fringe kind of person. She was the only person who tried to address women's issues on that course, discussing, for example, demographic changes and how we would have to get used to a lot more women entering the workforce. Many of the younger male students on the course completely rejected that idea. Once when a woman from Brighton Council came to talk to us on the course, it was terrible – the students were chatting right through her talk; she had a hearing problem and she had to stop and say, 'Look, I can't speak while you are all talking.' People actually got up and left while she was talking because they didn't want to hear what she was saying. It was that sort of atmosphere.

One of the lecturers on the HND course made misogynistic comments. He said several things that bothered me as well as another woman of about 30 who was there. In the seminar immediately afterwards, he made another really offensive remark so I said what I thought about this and he just replied, 'Well, some people have no sense of humour. You always get a couple of militants, don't you?' As it was, he subsequently made an apology to the group. So from that I came into doing Women's Studies and it was a really big change.

Going on the Women's Studies course is a bit like going back to school again. When I started the course I was a bit of a 'liberal feminist', very much into the equality approach, and I was very suspicious of a radical approach which validates 'femininity', which I saw as a form of weakness. I was very anti-essentialist but I've chilled out about that a bit – my views keep changing and developing.

Thinking Back: My Past, My Self

My mother comes from Sevenoaks and my father is from Trinidad. My parents were divorced when I was quite young and I haven't known my father for a lot of my life. My father was with us until I was about five but, strangely, I can't remember anything about him. My mother brought up myself and my siblings. More recently, I've begun to ask questions about myself and my father. There was a link with the Women's Studies course, which started to raise my awareness concerning my background from a race point of view. It was stimulated by the course; it made me think about my identity.

Last year there was a lecturer on my course who talked of a person who considered herself white but was mixed-race (Asian/white) and the lecturer found this really shocking. It made me realise that I hadn't really considered myself in 'colour' terms at all. It may be that I always felt more 'white' than 'Black', but then I knew I wasn't. So how I perceived myself was really confusing and I sometimes felt that the categories offered us in theoretical models don't always work. When I filled in the census form a couple of years ago I really didn't know how to describe myself. So I put myself down as 'other'. Sometimes I would like to belong to some nice little club, but most of the time I actually don't. Not belonging can make oneself a bit isolated. You can feel isolated because you don't really feel that you 'belong' anywhere. But at the same time that can be liberating, as you are not confined by any boundaries.

My mother has been absolutely essential to me. I am going through a second separation from my mother. I thought I'd separated from her the first time round, when I became an adult and moved away from home, but when I grew ill, that is when I had a breakdown, I was back in the same position as when I had been a child, of being at home and being cared for by her. I felt myself very tied to her, dependent on her.

My mother is very strong, though she just says she gets on with things because she just has to. I am quite strong, I am a coper, but that side of me disappeared for a while. I didn't move out again from home for two years. At present I see myself almost as being adolescent again and regard this as a new beginning. At least I very much hope it is.

I wonder if people that know me think I've changed a lot as a result of doing the course. I think I haven't changed that much; it's just consolidated a lot of things for me and has made me more articulate than I was before about women's issues. That was confirmed to me by someone who has known me for 15 years and who said, 'You've always been interested in these issues.' He didn't seem to think I'd changed that much. I am very aware of sexism, of having been treated differently all my life because of being female, and when I say 'differently', I don't mean better. When I was working as a model, for example, many men simply assumed that I was either stupid or a prostitute – otherwise, why be a model?

Being treated differently because of being a woman, which I've been aware of in my personal life, I now, through the Women's Studies course, have a format to discuss it in and people to discuss it with. My relationships with the people on the Women's Studies course are stronger than the ones I had on my previous course. There is only one person from that course that I am still in touch with, although I was with the same people for two years.

All this has had a big effect on me. I deal with sexism differently now. Things have changed for me over the last couple of years and Women's Studies has been a big part of that. I think I am no longer so willing to keep quiet about sexism.

At the same time I don't get so incoherently angry any more. I might be able to be slightly calmer and a bit clearer about rejecting a sexist stance without having to get into a raging row about it and without even understanding properly why. I used to suffer from a lack of confidence and I had a breakdown a few years ago. Both through things I've done outside the course and through the Women's Studies course, my confidence has grown. I have gained particularly in personal terms from the course. Academically, I was always fairly competent, but working hard can also be a way of hiding from problems – it's very easy to do that. On the Women's Studies course, paradoxically perhaps, I've been more comfortable with the ideas of not working for specific grades as such, of working because I enjoy it and knowing that I can make errors and that I can speak up in class and expose myself as something other than a hard-working student, as a person as much as a student. That, from my perspective, is unique to Women's Studies. There is more openness and fewer preconceived ideas about people and their performance. Therefore people are valued in a different way. It's been an extraordinary learning process for me.

We are encouraged to bring our personal experiences into the course and that, for me, was from the beginning one of the most interesting aspects of the course, going from being a slave to the objective to being encouraged to use 'I' in an essay, to write 'I think', was quite amazing. In the Business Studies unit I got into trouble: I had a little comment in the margin and my essay was marked down because I had supposedly given a 'too unbalanced view'. The topic was 'Rights and Justice in the Workplace', and I was told that I couldn't write about the Women's Movement because I'd done that for one of my seminars. That to me epitomised things on that course. If you'd written about or talked about women once, you couldn't do it again. I wouldn't like to think that I write completely from my own experience – of course I don't, because my experiences are already filtered through our culture, our language. I would think that my subjectivity in my essays is associated with my venturing an opinion on others' work, and that's why the Business Studies incident took me a bit by surprise because I thought I had done no more than that. I don't think I was being dogmatic.

Doing Group Work: the Tape-Slide Project

I've just been writing up a tape-slide project which to me epitomises what Women's Studies has done for me. For one thing, I wrote down, 'I am not "creative", I can't do this,' BUT I HAVE completed it. Also, I had worked in a group and I'd had it up to here with group work on my previous course. On the Women's Studies course we chose who we wanted to work with, and in my case I selected people who I felt I could work with and who, I thought, would have similar ideas about how to approach the work. Then we agreed on our subject matter. I hadn't known the other two women very well before starting the project. But I gained from working in this group and enjoyed it, AND did something that I really considered myself incapable of doing. So that was really brilliant. The group worked for me because I trusted the people I was working with. It may sound like a horrible cliché, but I felt that there was a sense of commonality between the people in my classes and myself, that we share certain values or aspirations or whatever you want to call them. It felt like we could trust each other and work together and gain from it. In other groups I haven't felt like that at all.

The project we chose was quite a personal one. We chose to work on our relationships with our fathers. I worked with two other people and it was a difficult topic for all of us. I barely could get through it, in fact. But that was productive. We all felt that we wanted to use the tape-slide project as an opportunity to do something personal. Doing it was an act of faith in a way: we wanted to combine utilising the facilities and environment we were in with something personal to us. This meant that we had to be prepared for this project to get public.

When I actually started working on it I got extremely cold feet about it – my father had died just over a year ago and I had just begun to get over it – but that was where the other people with whom I was doing the project came in and helped me to find ways to express my feelings about the project. Treating it as a project and there being another woman involved in the project who felt rather like I did really helped. By the end the whole thing had very much become a *project:* we had deadlines to meet, the work angle took over. But when we'd finished it, we started to worry again about who was going to see this. Until it's shown for the first time to a small group of fellow students and a couple of tutors, I don't know how we will feel about it.

The project fuses a personal narrative with some theoretical material. When it came to the making of the tape-slide the theoretical framing was added, but knowing about issues like 'the gaze' certainly informed how we did it. Our discussions of the project were not always theory-led. We got together at regular meetings to monitor each other's work and support each other.

The pieces were formed separately by each of us and put together towards the end. The meetings were therefore an opportunity for reflection and support from the other two.

Handling Subjectivity

Last year, I did a unit on 'The Manufacture of Madness' and I wanted to be a bit more subjective there and put in some of my experiences of therapy and so-called illness; having the label 'illness' used to describe me when I had my breakdown made me feel a lot better – afterwards, not at the time. But curiously, I found I couldn't bring myself to do it and I thought that it would invalidate the essay. I couldn't see a way of presenting arguments, writing an essay and bringing my experiences into it. I put a rough draft in and was told that it was all a bit vague – I just couldn't be specific.

One interesting effect of the Women's Studies course, though, has been that I look more critically at my therapeutic situation and now tell my therapist that I don't necessarily agree with her view of things. There can be conflict between the course and what happens in therapy and because the latter has been my anchor it has been difficult for me. The Women's Studies course has made me more critical and has enabled me to voice my disagreements with what I am being presented with in my own life. This is both destabilising and empowering.

Being Feminist

I'd like to think of myself as a feminist. I sometimes think that with Women's Studies there is something about being 'in the right club' and about 'being careful to be in the right club'. I feel that if I'm not, I'm letting the side down. It's nothing to do with the academic environment; I don't get the feeling from my lecturers that if I'm not in the 'right club' I get marked down or anything – it's outside of that sometimes, in other social contexts in which I don't want NOT to be seen to be pro-woman, a feminist, and I find myself thinking, 'Dare I say it?' Both in mixed-sex and in women-only contexts you get conversations where people end up being angry with you for saying what you think. I used to work in pubs and I got a reputation for being argumentative because I couldn't bear to hear what was being said.

Looking Ahead

Given the choice, I would definitely do the Women's Studies course again. But I wouldn't do both 'Women and Technology' units again, not because it wasn't interesting or useful but because there are all these other lovely things like literature and culture that I didn't think I could do – it has opened me to try new things – that course has definitely done that.

I've had conversations with people who say, 'What will happen when you get out into the "real world", when you have to try and work? It's all very well doing these courses full of ideas you agree with but what will happen afterwards?' The course has been empowering to the extent that it has enabled me to form opinions which are valid and which will stay with me on women's issues. Having said that, I am aware of the fact that my ideas are constantly developing. Some people think Women's Studies is cloud-cuckoo land and ask what is it going to qualify you for. But you could ask the same thing of other subjects such as English or Sociology that are not directly vocational. And similar answers pertain. Any potential employer who looks at my qualifications and says, 'What's the point of Women's Studies?' is not an employer for me. Basically, when a disempowered group such as women in this society claims space for itself and asserts its importance, it automatically gets attacked because it is challenging its status as disempowered.

5

Elspeth: Between Me and My Sister/s

Elspeth had a long history of involvement with women's groups and teaching Women's Studies without having a degree in that subject before becoming a Women's Studies student herself. Finding the late 1980s and early 1990s not like the 1970s, and that women on Women's Studies courses did not see themselves as feminists as a matter of course, she channelled her energies into learning how to make videos; the video she produced as part of her dissertation was about the relationship between herself and her sister. It fundamentally and positively affected that relationship.

Stops and Starts: Conservative and Radical

I was an undergraduate in 1957, when I went to Oxford and studied History. Before that I went to a convent, a very, very small school where no one else did even 'A' levels. I didn't do very well at Oxford. I had this difficulty with writing down what I assumed everyone already knew, the regurgitation aspect of it all, so I'd write very, very short answers and that wasn't OK.

I think I was very naive and young when I went there, having been at that very small school before and hardly meeting any other intellectuals at all. My father was a lawyer but not a very widely educated man, not a cultured person. So I was goggle-eyed to begin with and impressed by other people's credentials. My parents did not discourage me in what I wanted to do; I don't think they quite understood. I remember that when I got a third I was bitterly disappointed myself and I was also very upset that they didn't mind, that they thought that was fine. I am sure my parents were very proud of me, but I don't think they understood what it involved and what it meant. They didn't engage with the content or the ideas at all, and I wanted to be different from them. They were boring, insignificant people, everybody else had such glamorous parents – ambassadors and such like.

When I was an undergraduate I wanted to be a social worker. I don't think I was very ambitious or very confident. Compared with most of the other people, I was one of the timid ones. My first job was being an editorial assistant with *Encyclopedia Britannica*. Then I got a job at Dartington Hall School, which was a much more radical experience than being at university. I remember my mother saying, 'You've never been the same since you went to Dartington,' and she said that much more about Dartington than about going to Oxford. I was a part-time teacher there and a house-parent, so I had two jobs. It was there that I came across socialist ideas. I was very influenced by that place, although I was only there for two terms. Then I got married and got pregnant straight away, and went to the LSE and did a Diploma in Social Administration.

Having been at prestigious, traditional institutions has helped me in making changes in the directions I have made, especially the Oxford degree which is in many ways the least relevant of my qualifications. The period between getting married – I was 24 then – and ten years later is quite broken up. I did a lot of shifting, I had another son, then I worked in Essex for a year as a research assistant for someone who was doing history of architecture, and then I got a job with Peter Laslett here in Cambridge, working on the history of the family, in a group which was a radical, experimental group at the time, using quite elaborate statistics for historical analysis. That's what brought me to Cambridge. Then I applied to do a PhD and the History Department in Cambridge turned me down because I'd only got a third, I think, and/or possibly for political reasons. I don't know exactly why, but I was turned down and told to do an MPhil in Statistics at the LSE, which I couldn't stand at all. So I dropped that and reverted to social work. Then we moved to the village I now live in because of the school it has, and I started to work at the school, which was a radical place. It had an American headteacher, Beth Taylor, who was very student-centred and had Dartington-type ideas. I also started a training analysis to be a psychotherapist.

Initially, going into therapy had the disguise that I wanted to be a therapist. I genuinely thought I wanted to do that and felt confident that I would be good at it. But I lost faith in it. I was disillusioned with my motives because I decided that I did not want to help people all the time. Again, there was an element of the radical and the conservative. I started going to classic Freudian analysis sessions three times a week and simultaneously I got involved in co-counselling and encounter groups; that set up quite a lot of conflicts and I left the analysis after about 18 months, saying this is the most neurotic thing I do. Within that same time period, I started going to pottery evening classes, and there did seem to be a connection between the pottery and the encounter groups. They both had a creative feeling. Then I got a job in the student counselling service here. But we upped and went to New Guinea for a year because my husband – I had a husband then – had got a job there. We had, in fact, separated before that but we came together again.

The Women's Movement and the Beginnings of Women's Studies

In parallel with all that ran the Women's Movement and in 1969 I became very involved with the Women's Centre and con- sciousness-raising and a group of women. My confidence to make a proper break immediately after we came back from New Guinea came from that women's group. I remember thinking that it was OK to be by myself and to pursue my own thing, which is a curious thing to learn from political involvements. That's when I had the confidence to be 'selfish'.

I got involved in teaching Women's Studies through my teaching for the Open University on a course called 'Art and Environment', which is probably one of the most important things I've ever done. It was a very interesting course, very radical, much more radical than the Women's Studies course because it was radical in style *and* content, very much a 1970s course which had a very wide impact on a lot of students whose lives were changed by it.

I had also been peripherally involved when Cambridge University started a 'Women in Society' paper, which must have been in the mid-'70s. I ran some encounter groups among the people who were setting it up and among the first lot of students. These courses provided the academic context for my entry into Women's Studies. When I applied to teach Women's Studies for the Open University, they provisionally appointed four people but then found that they didn't have enough students. So they wrote to me, saying, 'Sorry, there aren't enough jobs,' and I did something I had never done before. I knew that one of the other appointed women was not going to stay in Cambridge for the whole of the academic year, so I rang her up and told her what the situation was and asked her if she would consider letting me take her place. That's how I started.

I felt I had a lot to give to the course because of the different kinds of teaching I had been doing. I feel very strongly that how you teach is as important as what you teach and I think that that's missing from Women's Studies, a shift in pedagogical methods. The ideas taught in Women's Studies often don't match how they are taught.

Women's Studies in the Academy: Studying after Teaching

The Open University course was one of the earliest in the country and I like being at the beginning of things. I'm not so good at sustaining – I like the buzz and the freedom when something hasn't quite jelled yet. I remember filling in forms when I was applying and feeling that my qualifications weren't academic enough. So I wanted a job that would give me those credentials.

I was part of the Women's Liberation Movement, though I didn't call myself a feminist then. Using that name only happened during the second or third year of the Open University Women's Studies course, and I was very resistant to becoming a 'feminist' because it was somehow respectable, it was institutionalising something which I thought should be outside. There's a really big conflict there for feminism. To me there was a problem with teaching Women's Studies within the patriarchal institution of the academy. Every person has to recognise what her compromises are in doing so. There's a conflict for me between wanting academic, that is institutional, validation on the one hand, and remaining free and outside the institution, on the other.

Wanting academic recognition has obviously influenced my doing the MA in Women's Studies. As someone said to me, 'You've already got an MA,' because, at Oxford, you automatically get one seven years after you've completed your BA, but it's also known that you don't have to work for that degree. It is quite odd in some ways that I'm doing this MA, because I've been teaching Women's Studies for so long. I am of course not familiar with everything in the field but I feel very, very familiar with a lot of the basic arguments and ideas. Therefore I've been very impatient on the course, but I've tried to suppress that. I've kept asking myself why I am doing this and the rational answer is that it's the opportunity to learn about video. That's what draws me to the course. That was something that I didn't already know about. I knew the people who were setting up the MA in Women's Studies and because of the video element I assumed the course would be radical.

Dreaming about Other Students

My expectations as to who would attend the course varied. I had
fantasy ones and realistic ones. My fantasy ones were about
radical feminists and us all sitting around discussing French
feminism, for example, very intensely. We would be existing in
some world which wasn't restricted and constrained in the ways
in which the actual institution is, partly in terms of people's
time. It was in part a fantasy of being a full-time student. But it
is a part-time course.

One of the things I wanted from the course was companion-
ship, and I've had that. I think I had a sort of a fantasy, though,
that I wanted something a bit like the early days of the Women's
Movement; I wanted a consciousness-raising group, with that sort
of intensity and commitment. And of course that wasn't what other
people wanted, so they didn't put it in. We have a subgroup who
meet in different ways and offer each other a lot of support. But
I think I imagined the whole group coming to the course with
that desire. But they were not coming with that kind of
commitment to the group as a group. They were coming to study.
They were interested in the issues, in women's writing or women's
history. But they said very adamantly that they didn't want to
get involved with the group, that they didn't have the time. It
wasn't a group experience they were after. They wanted to come
one evening a week and then they were going to study by
themselves. They treated Women's Studies very much like any
other academic discipline. In fairness, this didn't apply to absolutely
everybody, and there were a number of contradictions involved.
In fact, the woman I am thinking of in particular who said this
was also someone who frequently brought her own experiences
into discussions.

My more realistic and negative expectation was that I would
know more than a lot of the other students and that would raise
the question again of why I was doing it. I tried to prepare myself
for the possibility of that.

I nearly left after the first meeting because more than one
woman was saying that she wasn't a feminist, she was a human
being first, things like that. Because of the world I'd been living
in that seemed like an earlier stage somehow. I couldn't understand
why they wanted to do an MA in Women's Studies if they weren't
feminists, which was very naive, but I was really taken aback by
that and what that implied about their attitudes. It also indicated

the level of familiarity these women had with the literature. Of course, it wasn't realistic to expect that they should have much knowledge. Most of the women on the course had first degrees but clearly these degrees had no gender components in them. I have wondered many times since what keeps me going and I can only conclude that it has to do with the video, which I found very difficult to learn. Having made a video now, I can see that this became my reason for going.

'I Wasn't Very Good on the Course'

I have a feeling that I wasn't very good on the course, that I was very bad-tempered and didn't find a way of sharing the knowledge of Women's Studies I already had. That wasn't entirely my fault. I think there could have been a structure in which I could have shared it much more, but it was a taught course and the teachers were, on the whole, teaching, and not using the group as a resource. I don't think many of the teachers have experience of Adult Education; at least that's how it feels. I also suppressed a lot of what I did know because I felt that otherwise I would be taking over. There was one other person who was politically very engaged and was always quick to come in, and we made this vow to try and wait and leave space for other people. But we couldn't really sustain it. But that's a fairly negative solution and it would be interesting to know what other people thought. I felt that maybe I wanted to take over, so I stopped myself doing that.

I have stayed the course and my attitudes towards it have fluctuated quite a lot. My mother became very ill, so I missed a lot of sessions during the last term. At that stage, I think I temporarily took the more conventional line that I'd just have to do my work for the course and that was it because that was all I had time for. But much of the time I have fluctuated between thinking why am I doing this course, and a sort of excitement. I'd go to the sessions and get excited about the topic we were dealing with and then the following day have a very negative reaction of anticlimax and disappointment, thinking that we hadn't got anywhere and we were only just starting. Now it seems finished because the formal contact has finished and I've done the video. I feel more relaxed about it now because I've done the video and that was what I wanted to do.

Doing the video was different because it's a new medium for me and because I was barely in control of that medium. But that has nothing in particular to do with Women's Studies. There is a continuity between the way I did the video and how I did the other pieces of coursework. They are all verging on being art works. That's why I'm so pleased with the video, because it is not a conventional documentary. I am pleased with it because it is experimental and it worked. Technically it is experimental because it tries to overlap images a lot which is something I've done in still photography before, and it does it using very limited technical resources. You could do that comparatively easily with more and better resources, but given what was available to me it was very tricky. The video is also experimental in that it uses only visual material and does not have any spoken words in it. This is experimental in the context of an MA, though not in the context of film in general. I work in a very organic way, so I didn't know from the beginning that I was not going to use words, but as the video built up I could see that I didn't want to have words in it.

One of the ideas I was very interested in, and which Hélène Cixous writes about, is 'the economy of the gift'. The way in which I presented the video at the seminar was as a party. The video was wrapped up and passed around, and we took the layers off and played it. At one level the video came from outside the Women's Studies course in that it was about my sister and was a present for her. To me it therefore also represents very powerfully the idea of bringing the private into the public and then sending it back into the private again. I get a lot of pleasure out of making and giving presents.

'Between Me and My Sister': Sameness and Difference

The video is very much concerned with issues that are central to Women's Studies. It's called 'Between Me and My Sister' and it's about that relationship. It expresses the difference and sameness of sisters through a visual narrative. The thing that's most difficult about sisters and sisterhood is to retain the two, the sameness and the difference, and not to have to go to one or the other. This is what the video achieves. There's both affection and hostility in it. It isn't sentimental in any way, and yet it's not about a disaster or about insurmountable differences. It's affirmative but it's not soft – I hope.

It all started because I can't type, whereas Hilary is a very skilled typist. I suppose I must have had the inklings of something

because I asked her to help me with my first project, to type it.
The project was about lesbianism, and I was using it and the course
to talk to her about things I hadn't talked about with her before.
I remember thinking that she'll see what I've written, but she typed
it without reading it as such, which was quite funny. But I went
over and stayed the night and we talked a lot. I also had this sense
of acknowledging a skill she had, typing, which I didn't possess
but wanted. So there was an exchange of sorts. We talked about
my having relationships with women and, in making the video,
I realised that I had sexual feelings for her, which made me feel
very sad and also made me long to express it in some way. It was
very emotional and upsetting. It made me feel very attached to
her.

When I was making the video I thought a lot about the way in
which my relationship to the Women's Studies group was very
much like my relationship with my sister. My sister is completely
non-academic. She came up with this incredible thing I said to
her which she quoted back at me, saying that at some point in
the '60s I had told her to shut up when we were together in public
so that people wouldn't know how stupid she was. I don't
remember this but I'm sure it's true. I certainly thought it. I
dominated her through my intellect and she dominated me
through being much more attractive and socially successful. I can
see that some of that arrogance which I had towards her was present
in my attitude towards the Women's Studies group. When I
presented the video I think I was finally trying to share some of
my knowledge with the group. But to some extent the way I did
it had a bit of contrivance, show, controlling.

The group seemed to receive it very, very well. Hilary, my sister,
came. She had asked if she could do so, which was an extraordinary moment because I thought it was amazingly daring of her.
I don't think she quite saw it in that way – she was just interested.
But it was fascinating that she was there and her responses to the
video, which she hadn't seen until then, and to the questions asked
by the group, were interesting. Afterwards she said she was
depressed about it because she hadn't seen what other people were
seeing in the video; she was intimidated by the situation when
it happened.

The video has been amazing in terms of what has come out of
it, what people's reactions have been, making it, showing it to
her, her showing it to her family. It is very much part of my life
now and it has changed our relationship, shifted it enormously.
I feel much more open towards her now, much more at ease, less

disparaging. Those aren't the right words. What's happened is that I can see her qualities, who she is, how she is, and how we are the same. I find that very, very difficult and at the same time there's no getting away from it; it's visible. I've learnt an enormous amount from it all and although some of it has been painful for my sister, she has been very intrigued, very positive.

I think she and I experienced the division of beauty and brains very crudely. It had a great effect on me because I believed this crude version of things. It was like there was only room for these two possibilities. Somebody made an absolutely wonderful remark when we were in the pub after the showing of the film. I said that we were each afraid, one that the other was more beautiful, the other that the other was more brainy. And someone said, 'Oh, which was which?' This may have been sucking up or an outsider who didn't really know either of us very well and was genuinely not sure. But it was very interesting that it wasn't clear, especially in the context of me recognising Hilary's intelligence. I don't really think in those terms, the opposition of beauty and brains, any more now, I don't really think that I'm unattractive. At least it's not as near the surface as it used to be, it doesn't rankle anymore.

My Sense of Self

My sense of self-validation comes from how I see myself in academic terms. I keep pretending to myself that I'm mystified about why I am staying on the course because I don't want to know that I am still trying to get validation that way, because another bit of me is very dismissive about it and not interested in it. What was painful in making the video and what was also painful about the course, the thing about being arrogant, is that it raised the question of why I am doing it. It is also difficult to reveal all this as possibly true about oneself. What I have noticed is that whenever I've gone up the next stage in my work as a potter, I have a long break and go off and do an MA or photography or whatever.

One thing the course has done for me is introduce me to a lot of new and interesting reading. I like the work of Donna Haraway and of Judith Butler. I've also read a lot more of Hélène Cixous' work, which I found interesting both academically and in relation to creativity. It renewed my interest in the concept of creativity. It feels like food for sustaining and encouraging my own thinking. Although it may be hard to see in my pots, I am actually very stimulated by words and language. I don't think I would enjoy pottery as much as I do if in some way I did not feel that I put words into it. It has also been very interesting for me working in two dimensions rather than three. Two dimensions are somehow closer to words. It seemed a lot more difficult to make a video than to make pots. It's more treacherous, there are more pitfalls. It seems harder to get across what you want to say.

I am not sure that there is a specifically 'feminine' artistic voice. Some works by men are as powerful to me as work by women. At the same time I feel that some of my most powerful work comes out of being a woman, out of having a female body, which is biologically female and has been socialised to be female. I stopped menstruating about three years ago and when I had a stray period a couple of weeks ago, it was the most extraordinary sensation.

I genuinely feel an incredible ambivalence towards established power and recognition and what that means. It seems to involve a lot of compromise. At the same time, I continue. Given how late I started, I've been very successful and I can see that with another personality I could be even more so, but I hover just below that and something in me doesn't want it. I seem to dart in and out again. I like that position.

Someone once asked me was I afraid of success, but I thought, 'No, you're wrong.' It is a genuine ambivalence which I don't want to resolve. When I had an exhibition of my pottery in the most important gallery for this kind of work in London, I made the pots and then went to London with some completely new work, and the curator said that she couldn't have the new pieces in the show. I had the exhibition of the known work, as it were, but she did not want the new work, this development. I wanted that question in this exhibition. It wasn't possible. You're expected to repeat yourself. For whatever reasons I like to define myself as more wriggly, more on the move than that.

Breaking the Mould

If I was running an MA in Women's Studies I would regard it as part of the course that students must devise their own course. This is, of course, utopian, in that I know there would be incredible difficulties in getting a course like that validated. So perhaps I am saying that the kind of pedagogy, structure and practice I would like would be something necessarily defined by the particular group of women doing the course. The idea would be that you find out what it is you want to learn and then you find out how to find that out. You do that through a dynamic interactive process. But if you have a more conventional framework in existence, I think there's still scope for a much more responsive, interactive, improvisatory position on the part of the teacher, so that the teaching is a time for provocation, stimulation and offering pointers and it's not a time for the transfer of information *per se*. It requires a teacher who likes being scared, who likes beginnings, because every session you're at the beginning. The preparation for it is different from how you prepare for the delivery of information. You may prepare to be the devil's advocate sometimes and someone who questions everything.

What militates against that happening is the expectations of teachers and students who have a model in their head of how teaching operates which is conventional. If you want to break that mould you have to do it consciously, and both students and teachers have to agree to do that. You have to have a plan. If the teacher wants it to happen she can suggest it to the students, so teacher desire plays a big role.

Being a Feminist

Being involved in Women's Studies for ten years, both teaching and studying, has influenced me. When I hear myself talking, at my sister's, for example, I realise that I have a whole series of assumptions which are feminist as well as academic. It's almost hard for me to see the extent to which I am steeped in it all. Being a feminist means making that claim over and over again because it isn't accepted, it isn't a foregone conclusion, even in Women's Studies. I find that quite alarming. One assumption I tend to make is that a woman is an independent person with a commitment to other women who will also make a commitment to you. I think I'm quite old-fashioned in that I was a feminist before I got involved in Women's Studies and it does not occur to me to theorise my position in the first instance; that comes second. I live it first, which is why the first day of the Women's Studies course was so disappointing. 'Feminist' is the only ideological label that I have ever taken on, though I was a Christian once as a young child. But I haven't ever belonged to a political party or anything like that. My being shocked at women declaring themselves to be non-feminist is partly to do with the fantasy I was having and partly a function of my age and lack of contact with younger women. I don't see so clearly what's happening now compared to 20 years ago. But I have also lost some of the energy I used to invest in feminism.

Being over 50 and one of the oldest women on the course has had considerable bearing on my experience of it. There was one other woman with adult children and another one who'd been very much involved in the Women's Movement, which meant that she and I shared a lot of historical references. My age did give me a feeling of separateness and I wanted the others to be the same age, to be companions. In a way it was a bit like trying to go back into the past. The fact that I was familiar with a lot of the material and debates was possibly a hindrance to others rather than to me.

I feel I have to do something completely different now. I am showing my video in a number of contexts and I have a familiar sensation of putting myself forward in a new world and wondering what will happen. I am neglecting the pots and I don't really like doing that. I also don't like some of the practicalities of making videos, such as sitting for hours and hours in the dark. On some level I can't imagine doing that sort of thing for a long time and I can't quite see the context for it.

If I had my time over, I am not sure I'd go on the course again. I might like to learn making videos in a more video-oriented environment, which I might have found more stimulating than the MA in Women's Studies. The video-related skills aspect of that course, which was new to me, was the best bit on the MA, as well as the effect it had on my relationship with my sister. Maybe that could have happened without the video, but I don't think I could have involved my sister if it hadn't been a Women's Studies course.

6

Chris: From Sciences to Women's Studies

Chris, coming from a sciences background, had to give up her career in teaching as a result of ill health and took up Women's Studies to effect a complete break with her past.

A Metamorphosis

I was 48 when I started the MA in Women's Studies. There were lots of personal reasons for coming on the course. I wasn't working at the time due to illness. I was at a stage where I didn't quite know what I was going to do with myself; I had to deal with my problem of no longer being able to go to work, and had to find something that would interest me and give me something to do.

I saw the advert for the course in the paper, and thought it looked interesting. Being nearly 50, being a woman and a mother, and having gone through quite a lot of experiences seemed an appropriate basis for doing the course. Also, it was very different from what I had done before. Because of the situation I was in – early retirement due to ill health – I felt that if I did something completely different it would be so new and fresh that it would help me deal with where I might go in the future.

It was like a complete break with my past. I feel like I am going through a metamorphosis – I use the word metamorphosis because it means something for me; it has to do with changing things, with change in myself. I've gone through a couple of these before, but this is a really big one and I think I am going to come out a rather different person from how I started, for a variety of reasons. I saw the course as an opportunity to start afresh.

An Alien Species

I was quite scared when I first attended the course. I was really put off in the first couple of sessions because I felt like an alien species, primarily because everyone around me was talking about the arts and poetry and things that I didn't really know much about and which hadn't really been part of my life. I felt that I was a tremendous outsider; it rather put me into a position of feeling very inferior, very scared, and wondering whether this was the right thing, whether I should have dared do this, and should I chuck it in now and do something I felt more comfortable with. The first few weeks were hell on earth really; then I decided that I wasn't going to allow anyone or anything to determine what I did and I was going to see it through, whatever. So I stuck it out, and came out the other side.

Sometimes I am quite content being in a group but simultaneously being a bit outside it. I don't mind that too much. Other times it may matter a lot. On the Women's Studies course I was in and out. I've been quite independent, because many times in my life I've done things on my own as I had to and therefore being on my own is not a real problem.

During the process of doing the group project we had some moments of extreme annoyance because, for example, we had made a decision to meet at a particular time and someone just couldn't bring herself to get up in time. I decided to keep my counsel on that one; there was a lot of discontent and I felt that if I voiced my views too strongly, it would only exacerbate things and disrupt the group further. So I just let it go, and we all stayed a lot longer to finish the group project.

I found I had to hold back within the study groups. I liked being asked to read texts and took issue with some of what I read, but I did not always feel able to discuss my views the following week, or particular points that I was interested in weren't picked up in the general discussion.

I think I've always felt slightly different from other people – mostly I can handle it and I don't let it bother me too much. I tend to think that we are all different and that there's a lot of value in that. When we did the group project our various different perspectives helped to introduce variety. It is important that everyone accepts all these diverse perspectives. You can get a great deal from that.

We arrived at working well together but immediately after we'd presented the project, the study group instantly and utterly collapsed. That was incredibly disappointing because I felt that those of us who had stuck together to keep the thing going when it could have all just blown apart prior to that, had in a way worked at it for nothing – it all fell apart afterwards anyway. People seemed to think that there was no real purpose to the group after the project. But various women had given a great deal to the project and gone through a lot with it, so it felt like the project should not have been the end of it all. I stayed friends with only one other woman from the study group – we kept on meeting. It was a pity that we never used the study group time properly again.

I am not sure how I saw myself when I started on the course; whether I saw myself as a feminist, for example. Depends how you define 'feminist', of course. My attitude towards feminism changed during the course. I took on board many of the issues raised by feminism. I don't think you can go through a course like Women's Studies without positioning yourself somewhere or other. It's a kind of evolution. I've changed a lot.

Because I'd gone through experiences of how badly women are treated, especially in the workplace, I had strong views about that. In school, as a teacher, I had a particular head who was an autocrat, very paternalistic. His view of women was that women worked for pin money. If you looked at the structure of the school he set up, all the women were at the bottom of that structure, and many of the weak males were way above the women in position, riding on the backs of the women who occupied the lower ends of the scales. I was one of those at the time, and it was always a great bone of contention among the women in the staff room, with comments such as, 'Look at that drip – can't even organise a piss-up in a brewery.' At the time, there were 22 departments in the school and there was only one female head of department – needless to say, that was Home Economics, because of course no male ever taught it so there were no male feet in the department. I was the only female scientist at the school for a couple of years with just men around me and I had quite a battle on my hands with some of these men. I was very miffed that they were promoted whereas the women weren't, but that was the head's deliberate policy.

The Only Woman

When I was at college I was the only woman doing sciences way back in 1959 to 1964. Initially, there were a couple of other girls around but they dropped out and eventually I was the only one left. My background is such that I was the only girl, with three elder brothers. My father died when I was four and my eldest brother was killed ten months later, so my mother had to cope with two bereavements in ten months.

I was the only daughter. My two remaining brothers went off to a charity boarding school for widows when they were eleven and I was left at home with my mother. She worked all day as a cleaner mopping other people's floors and so forth because, coming from a middle-class background, she was a nanny before she got married so she had no training for a different job, and in any event after the war it was very difficult for a woman of her position to get work. I was very upset as a child because I didn't have a father; luckily for me there were quite a lot of children at school who also didn't have a father because they were killed in the war. My father wasn't killed in the war; he died of a brain tumour. So, although I wasn't on my own in not having a father, nevertheless I always felt I had missed out somehow.

As a child, I was always crazy about sciences, very bright, very mathematical. That interest was stimulated before grammar school. At the time of his death, my father was studying to be a pathologist, and there were all these books of his around in my bedroom. My mother never threw them out so they were left there, all these books on physiology and such, and I used to read them as a child. I felt these were for me somehow. As I became seven, eight, nine, I used to read these books; they were a great love of mine, as was Maths, which I was very good at.

At the age of ten I passed the eleven plus and went to grammar school. There was a bit of controversy because the local grammar schools were single-sex, and at the girls' school they didn't teach separate sciences, so I didn't want to go there. I made it quite clear to my mother that I wasn't going to go there – I wanted to go to the one ten miles away which, very unusually, was a co-educational school. There were virtually none of those around then. I had found out that they taught separate sciences there, Chemistry, Physics, Biology; I didn't know what these wonderful subjects were but that was what I wanted. So I virtually made my mother allow me to go to this school – and she did. She did everything she could in her ability – she had no money, of course, but she supported me. So I went to this school and, lo and behold, it had separate sciences. The Chemistry teacher there was an eccentric and I thought he was wonderful; he walked around in his bow tie with all the chemicals laid out in front of him, allowing us to experiment, change colours of liquids and so on. I loved it. I thought Physics much more boring than Chemistry.

Then I made a great mistake in my options. I'd got very interested in languages and when the option came up I chose Latin, which meant I couldn't do Biology. I didn't realise until many years later that this would have consequences for what I could study. There was no careers advice at school, no one to make you understand what certain choices implied. It was just hit and miss.

When I got to 16, my mother couldn't afford to keep me on at school. She could hardly afford the uniform, never mind anything else. I accepted the situation, that I'd have to leave school. So I got a job in a local research lab, and went one day a week to take my 'A' levels in Maths, Physics and Chemistry. I worked at the same time as studying. Eventually, I got a degree from the Royal Institute of Chemistry. That's how I became a works chemist, as it was called. Then, 15 years later, after I'd been at home with the children for a while, I did another degree in Earth/Environmental Sciences. So I had an all-sciences background.

In a work situation I never met another woman doing chemistry. I liked being the only woman. The boys at college were very nice to me. At work there was some discrimination. Once I was told to go and act as a driver at work when I was the works chemist, to go and pick something up from somewhere over 100 miles away. So I asked to speak to the manager and told him that I was not prepared to do this.

The Shock of Seeing My Self

I spent seven years getting to the position of works chemist. I got married and continued to work until I got pregnant, when I stopped work one month prior to my daughter's birth. We are talking about the early 1960s now, when it was expected that women stayed at home once they had children. So I expected that but did not realise the implications of it at the time. I knew my job would go and I would be a wife and mother. It was only later that it hit me what all this meant. I had two children very quickly; that was my choice, and it was fine.

Then the problems started because the second child was a very difficult baby. He never slept. He was one of these hyperactive children who walked very early on. Additionally, things were very tight financially: we had a first house, two babies, one income ... It was a combination of many factors, but because for two years the baby never slept I could never sleep, always having to rescue him from getting bags of flour out of cupboards at two in the morning, that sort of thing. So, I was reduced to being stuck at home with two small kids, no sleep, little money, what appeared to be not much fun and a great deal of drudgery, and no pre-knowledge of what all this meant. I had also moved away from my family at the time, which meant I had no friends as such immediately around me. I had to go and find friends, having left those I'd had at work behind.

This then resulted in endless cups of tea and biscuits, which was the only thing I could afford. My waistline expanded; I got huge. I put on about six stone. In the end I wouldn't go out because I was so ashamed of myself. My husband never said anything about it. His life had changed drastically, too. He now had all this responsibility, trying to support a family, with two children and a house.

I resolved it in the end. I had a letter to post one day. At the time I had a huge navy blue gaberdine raincoat which went virtually down to my ankles and certain Hush Puppy shoes which were the only shoes I could get into – I can see them now. The raincoat had a hood. Because I wasn't going out at the time on account of being so ashamed of my size, I waited until the evening post at six o'clock when it would be dark and I could sneak out of the door and be unseen, like a ghost in the night.

There was a mirror by the front door which my husband used to check himself in before he left in the morning. I didn't usually look at myself in this mirror by the door because I did not want to reveal to myself that I was this ugly amorphous blob, which is what I was. But I did see myself at that point as I was going out of the door and I was terribly shocked because I saw how other people must see me. I had avoided this recognition before. But I saw this image and I was very shocked and shaken because I was much worse than I had perceived myself to be.

I knew I was fat and horrid and ugly but I didn't realise quite how fat until I saw myself in the mirror. This shook me rigid. So I went out to post the letter and on the way I decided that I had to do something about this, I just couldn't continue as I had done. I dealt with it by going on a very strict diet. I also saw a notice in the post office to start a new women's group in the area, so I decided to join it and I went along to the first meeting. Subsequently, I became the chairwoman of that group. This wasn't a Women's Institute group; the whole point of it was that it was for young women, new to the area, who hadn't any friends, and I was one of its inaugural members. I joined the group, and lost all that weight in about 22 weeks.

This then was reflected in my personality change, which was very noticeable. Prior to my huge state, I had been an extrovert and very gregarious. But I had become an introvert, introspective and morose. By shedding five and a half stones, I refound my personality. My husband noticed that, that I was getting back to being like I had been all those years ago before we were married. He commented on my returning to my former self, that I was now who I really was, that while I had been so fat I had been somebody else, not me. In some ways that was true but obviously I was me, even during that very fat phase, but I came in a different guise.

A Chance to Be Me/A Chance to Be Different

The women's group was very important to me because it gave me social contacts and allowed me to have – legitimately, let's put it that way – evenings away from home and family, which helped me to go out, shut the door and have a rest from worrying about the kids. It gave me a chance to be me. I think I saw it as my time, without any guilt that I was not at home.

With four children, two girls and two boys, I developed a strong sense that I did not want to be like my mother, specifically I did not want to be left unexpectedly to look after four children with no means of support like she had been. She was extremely poor. So at about 37 I began the degree in Earth/Environmental Sciences to become a teacher, as this fitted in best with my family commitments. My four kids were between five and 14 then.

I also did not want my daughters to be like me, never really doing what they wanted to do. Their education was central to me, partly because my mother had not been able to support me through the whole of my own education, and partly because I had seen as a child what poverty and being unemployable as a female can mean. I wanted my daughters to be as highly educated as possible and to be employable on decent salaries. I wanted them to be able to *choose* what they did, so that if they had chosen to get married and have children at 21 – which I did not particularly want them to do – that would have been fine, but neither of them did. With the boys I always felt they'd be OK anyway, they were boys and would, just for that reason, be able to do what they wanted. But for girls it's different. So I encouraged the girls to do what they wanted to do, at the expense of my time. I feel quite proud of them and of myself in that, if we could afford it, they had it or did it. We have a bit of a joke about it now in the family, with me saying, 'Look at all the things you were able to do that I couldn't because I was a war baby.' I suppose in some ways I see my daughters as an extension of myself, doing what I couldn't do.

When I came on the MA in Women's Studies, a different set of issues were in play. My time had been given back to me, unexpectedly, because I was suddenly no longer working, which was not my decision. I had been thrown into this situation where I had a lot of time on my hands, and I had to decide how to deal with that time. I had a lot of it all of a sudden, having been in full-time work before, with more and more responsibilities, and moving up the career ladder. I had been head of department; I was on the senior management team, and there was a future which would fill the time I would have once all the children left home to go to university. That was how I had visualised it – but it didn't happen like that.

When I came to the Women's Studies course I had no idea of what the outcome of my illness was going to be – would I be able to drive, for example – so I had to find something to do within the vicinity of where I live. One of my sons was also still at home. I looked at all sorts of things apart from the MA in Women's Studies, but none of them appealed to me. I didn't want to be negative about what I was going to do in the future and hang on to the past. I tend not to hang on to the past. Lots of times in my life I've had to let go and I have done. When I arrived on the course it was a time of letting go. I wanted to do something completely new, something so new that it would become completely absorbing, which would stop me dwelling on my situation. I homed in on Women's Studies because it did not seem to have terribly rigid parameters; I felt it would allow me to find something that would really interest me. I liked the breadth of the discipline, and the freedom it suggested for me to pursue what was of interest to me – that seemed to me to be the strength of the subject. I saw its possibilities, which I assumed rather than knew of at the time, and this assumption was confirmed. Women's Studies opened my eyes to lots of interesting things that I might have dismissed at one time. It opened a new world to me, not because there was anything wrong with the world I was inhabiting but because it was different. It provided me with a whole new set of dimensions for the way I look at things.

I still have a great interest in sciences – I am interested in the why and the how of things. The sciences have a very profound effect on how I see the world, so that I think I see things very differently from how other people see things. I don't say this to many people, as they might find it alienating. Taking back science to cosmology and creation and how things arrive in the world is interesting to me. Natural things such as wood and stones are not just surfaces – when I look at them and think about them as beautiful and what that means, I think about how these things work underneath, their molecules and structures, why they are a particular colour and so forth. A piece of wood is not an inanimate object to me because it contains energy, vibrational energy; it is a weak energy but it is there, so it has force. I see things in those terms.

New Experiences

I got a lot out of the course – many different things, really. It opened my eyes to many things that I'd never thought about before. It was outside of anything I'd ever experienced before. I had shut the door on my past life and this was like another door, a beginning again.

I was very interested in the cultural studies side of things rather than the sociological aspects that I had come across before. There were many women authors I'd never heard of, never read before. I liked *Days* by Eva Figes a lot. I am ruthless about books – if I get impatient with them, I have no qualms about rejecting books, not finishing them. In fact I do a lot of rejecting rather than accepting, and I accepted *Days*. It was a book about a woman starting in hospital which at the end begged the question of was she alive or dead; I found the process of disclosure and acceptance, the woman coming to terms with what had happened to her, interesting – had she undergone a metamorphosis? I did not think she had died at the end, though lots of other women on the course did – I thought she had gone through a process of disclosure, recognition and acceptance out of which the woman came a whole person. That's how I understood it.

I enjoyed doing the coursework. Being able to pursue our own areas of interest was an aspect I really enjoyed and had never experienced before. While I liked being able to choose the topics myself, I did wonder how, given that we were all working on very different things, this coursework could be marked fairly. That's to do with my scientific background. I found that hard to imagine. My view was that the person reading an essay they were interested in might be affected by this. In science, especially at school, you mark in a 'this is right' or 'this is wrong' way, in objectively quantifiable ways. We had some discussion on the course about this.

For my dissertation I wanted to do something that was important to me. I did some work on all-inclusive language in the church, the development of services that include women as well as men in their address. At the time, the language of the church bothered me. I had not thought through the issues other than to be aware of the fact that there was something wrong from my perspective. This had been there for years. The Women's Studies course gave me the opening to pull out something that had been hanging around as an irritation for a long time. So I tried to work out if there really was a problem. When we talked about language and gender on the course, I began to see why I had felt uneasy in relation to the church. That formed the basis of my dissertation. The issue was, why did I always feel so excluded in the service situation at church, why did I feel that nobody was talking to me, what was I doing there – so it started with personal experience. I realised that I was feeling excluded because of the language of the church. Up until we started to look at language on the Women's Studies course, I had never tried to work out what I found so unsettling at church. So looking at language enabled me to resolve that issue. You could say that the course gave me the vehicle to understand what had been part of my discontent. This was the answer.

I'd do the course again, but there might be other aspects that I would now be interested to hear more about than we covered on the course. I would like to go on to work much more on issues such as women and science, women in religion in the broadest sense, topics we never really dealt with on the course but that I explored by myself a bit.

7

M: Cross-cultural Moves

M is an Argentinian woman who came to Britain in the late 1960s. Doing an MA in Women's Studies in the early 1990s as a 'mature' student brought to the surface for her issues about feminism in the 1990s, identity and cross-culturalism.

Arriving in Britain from Argentina

I came to live in Britain in 1971. I spoke English and I had been here before for a year in 1968 when I was 18 and arrived to study English. I didn't do what I was supposed to do – though I attended some courses I was interested in: I did a course on phonetics at Edinburgh University during the summer, for example. But mainly I did a lot of other things, travelling around a lot in Europe, meeting people from different countries, making friends and going to theatres, cinemas and art galleries.

My father encouraged me to develop myself when I was at home. He always wanted me to study and to travel; when I came to Britain in 1968 my mother wasn't happy about me coming on my own. She may have had fears of losing me – but she never said anything to me about going back or put any pressure on me once I came to live here with my husband (who is British). My mother has a very traditional down-to-earth attitude; she looks at her life in phases, her children being at home was one phase, my going away another, she's a grandmother now.

My grandparents were immigrants, Spanish mainly; my father was born in Bolivia but grew up in Argentina; the generation of my grandparents were mainly European who went to Argentina because things were difficult in Europe for some of them.

My grandparents acquired land, and my mother was brought up in the countryside. She did not complete her secondary education. I have one aunt – out of four sisters – who left her home town to go to Cordoba to attend university. At the time it was quite a big thing to do for a woman. She became a dentist. In my mother's family my mother is the only daughter who got married; the other three sisters didn't, which was unusual at the time because women were supposed to be housewives and mothers. I don't think it was because of lack of opportunity. It may have had to do with certain attitudes towards sexuality or experiences they had. I don't know.

I went back to Argentina in 1968 and worked, teaching English. I returned in 1971 and got a place at Essex University, but I didn't have a grant and my husband and I had various financial problems. I think it was also too soon for me to do a degree course, having just arrived to live in this country. In 1968 I had been a tourist, travelling around a lot. I did not have the awareness and under-standing of this society I developed once I came to live here. I was pretty naive. When I went back to Argentina at the end of '68 people would ask me about aspects of Britain, the weather for example, and how people coped and I used to say, 'Well, all houses have central heating.' So it was quite a shock – when I came to live here in 1971 – to discover that this wasn't so as a matter of course.

After a while I did a Cert. Ed. for two years, as I had teaching experience from Argentina, and then I got a job with the Social Services, which I did for a year until my daughter was born. I then stopped working for three or four years, and when my son was very young I began to go to some seminars on feminist theory and feminist issues at a local university. I found that very interesting and I went every Wednesday, leaving my son in a creche. By that time, 1983, I was no longer politically naive. I was involved in general left-wing politics through my husband. We had been involved in the Chile Solidarity campaign and had had a refugee staying with us. My husband had a more active and 'public' role than I. It was all quite new and I was learning a lot, but I was also very aware of being a woman and being treated differently. Gender issues seemed more relevant to my life.

The Women's Group

I'd been thinking about doing Women's Studies for a long time before I came on the MA course two years ago. I'd got some information about similar courses in London, for example, but the one I attended in the end was near to where I live so that seemed just right.

Previously, I had been involved in a women's group which we started in 1981. I found out about it through *Spare Rib*. I was introduced to *Spare Rib* by my husband, who was at Sussex

University in the early 1970s. At first I didn't read *Spare Rib* terribly regularly, but then I went through a phase when I did.

Somebody wrote an advert in *Spare Rib*; it gave a phone number in a small semi-rural town, which amazed me, so I contacted this woman who lived in the middle of a rural area near that town and she arranged a meeting. Seventeen women turned up to the first meeting – we all thought that this was amazing for an area like the one we lived in. That was the start of the group. At the time I did not think of it as a consciousness-raising group, but afterwards I realised that it had been. We used to meet every Sunday – religiously, I always use that word – in the evening, and we discussed all sorts of things, such as our personal experiences of sexism, our upbringing, our relationships with men, being 'mothers' ... We also used to go to the theatre together; we went to a national women's conference in London; we organised a seminar on 'Feminist Perspectives' in conjunction with the WEA and a university nearby.

The group was very important for me. Most of us in the group were young mothers with small children, but there also was a 16-year-old woman who was still at school and one or two women who did not have children. It was a very important experience for all of us. We were together for two years. Then it began to disintegrate, though I kept in touch with two or three of the women. Afterwards I joined another group in another small town nearby, but it was never the same again ... The group didn't work in quite the same way; it disintegrated much sooner – though, again, I've kept in touch with some of the women from that group.

Fantasy and Reality

When I came to the MA in Women's Studies, my main interest was in Women's Studies rather than in a degree. I wanted to learn more about the issues that I had begun to explore with the women's group. It wasn't necessarily the degree that was of interest; even if there hadn't been the piece of paper at the end I would have done it just the same, exactly as I did when I went to the Wednesday seminars before. I wanted to find out more.

When I arrived on the course I wanted to meet lots of exciting women. I thought I would meet many feminists and that things would 'happen'; I would get involved in groups and we'd become so strong and there'd be so much energy that we would be able to go out and do things. That was the fantasy. I wanted the opportunity to explore myself and issues, take risks. We don't know what we are capable of, what our potentials are, until we go out and try things, but it is much easier to do that in a group. I expected women who would be questioning our position in society, women who had been in other consciousness-raising groups as well, who were willing to discuss feminist issues. I expected some sort of activism; I had no clear, set ideas but I was hoping that I'd get inspired.

I've always been interested in artistic things, for example, but I've never developed that side of myself. I remember being told at the first meeting of the Women's Studies course about the group project and the dissertation, the different ways in which one might develop and present these, so I thought this would offer an opportunity for me to try out that side of my self. That's just one aspect. It could have been something more political that was developed. That was the fantasy. I think I was stuck in the '70s.

The reality was of course different, though whatever happens on the course is all learning. There were women on this course who did not know that such a thing as Women's Studies existed prior to coming on the course, or who had come to the course because it was an MA. Again, I suppose I had not taken on board the general climate, the effects of Thatcherism. Also, one expects other women to have had a similar history as oneself. It was the functionalist approach, the fact that for some women it could have been any other MA, that I found difficult to accept.

My study group worked very well and we built up trust very easily, but after we'd done our group project it fell apart – the whole experience had been very task-related. The project had to be presented at a certain date and that's what dominated people's thinking. Without the task we would not have had that focus. People's motivation is an important factor.

I was confused and disappointed when I realised that not all the women on the course were feminists. I began to think about myself. I was reading interesting, new material – so that was that. At least I was getting something out of it. There were many aspects of feminism that I hadn't come across before; some were connected with issues I had been interested in for a long time, to do with language for example, or to do with ethnicity. When it came to doing the dissertation and the essays we had to write, both gave me an opportunity to look at areas that meant a lot to me in terms of learning. So I wrote about the Mothers of the Plaza de Mayo, for example, and my dissertation has to do with Latin American women. I am using this opportunity to investigate issues that are important to me personally. Trying to look at myself in an academic context is very exciting, but I feel isolated because there is not much sharing of ideas.

Questions of Identity

I am aware that there is much more to learn. I am trying to explore questions of identity at the moment; that is quite an important area for me right now. There are other ones which I'd also like to look at, such as sexuality, which I didn't work on much on the course. For example, I haven't really read much about lesbianism. Perhaps this should be addressed more on the course – though we did have Celia Kitzinger come and give a talk.

It would also be better if the course did not have such a Eurocentric perspective. The group with whom I'm working for my dissertation is a group of Latin American women living in Britain. Their 'origin' and national identities is an important aspect of my work. But I am also exploring our identity as women. I identify with the women in the group because of the cultural points of reference which we share, aspects of Latin American culture that have made me what I am. There is a certain amount of nostalgia involved in that but that is not what interests me predominantly; it's the use of language, certain 'poetic', witty ways of looking at things which perhaps I have neglected. I think all the women in the group, including myself, are at different points of assimilation or 'translation', which is interesting to consider because it means that we have to negotiate our lives here (and in Latin America) in very specific and different ways. For me it's important to use Spanish in this group; in fact it's the only opportunity I have to use my original language. Also perhaps there are the possibilities at some point in the future of doing some work about Latin American women.

Women's development in Latin America is different in some respects from that of women in Britain. The question of class comes into this, and I am talking about it from a middle-class perspective. The situation of women growing up in Latin America cannot be divorced from the politics of Latin America and the impact that this has on everyday life and everybody. I left Argentina and escaped much of that, but many of the women from the Latin American group have been affected directly by political events in Latin America. Some of them had to leave their countries, some were arrested, detained, experienced torture. Others left because they were threatened or because they saw the political climate getting worse. I missed all that and it's funny because I've always felt a tinge of guilt about it, somehow I feel I should have gone through all of that too.

I got involved with the Latin American Women's Group because I got to know somebody who was in the group, and the idea of meeting other Latin American women attracted me, but at the same time one of my tutors suggested that I might do a dissertation about that group. I found doing the two things very difficult. With hindsight it might have been easier if I had met the women first, got to know them and then decided, yes I will do this or not. As it was I felt I had to say at the first meeting what my double interest in the group was. I don't think I could have done anything else, given the time factor.

Personal Concerns

My experience of the Women's Studies course as a course was good. I felt we needed a lot more time for discussion but I enjoyed the lectures, some more than others of course. In the end it was up to us as students to get as much out of the course as we wanted. The opportunities were there; it was up to us to take them. We discussed personal experiences in small groups, for example, but the sort of discussion I wanted was of a more academic nature, because I lack confidence at that level. That didn't happen, because people needed to talk about what they were going through, and that takes time. Maybe that has to do with people's motives for attending the course. It meant that they chose mainly to focus on personal concerns and perhaps did not feel the need to explore academic issues verbally. Often people reacted negatively to an attempt at that kind of discussion.

In many ways I think that perhaps this has to do with a very British attitude towards being an intellectual, which I am always aware of because I compare it with the Argentinian situation. For historical and colonial reasons, the ethos of 'doing well' was connected with being educated, having a degree, having been to university, etc. That, plus the role of the intellectual in Latin America, means that education has a higher status there than in Britain. Apart from the British anti-intellectual attitude, there was always a gender angle: women feeling threatened or vulnerable, particularly at the beginning, about someone else 'knowing' more or having read more.

Even so, I learnt a lot while I was on the course about the development of feminism in the last decades, for example, and the question of difference. I came across various women writers – such as bell hooks, Julia Kristeva, Liz Stanley – that I hadn't heard of before. I hadn't really read about Black feminism before coming on the course, or about postmodernism, orientalism, Italian feminism and so on.

My Self

I align myself with all sorts of positions; I don't think I align myself with any particular feminist position all the time. In this society I float between seeing myself as marginal and as central. By and large I have not felt marginalised although lately, at work, I have felt differently at times because of the general climate of insecurity and the status of Adult Basic Education – which is what I do – in a college of further and higher education.

The day that the National Front candidate was elected in Tower Hamlets, I went into a shop and accidentally bumped into a woman who then became extremely angry and abusive. I am sure she muttered something like 'wog ...'. It didn't affect me at all; in fact I understood her somehow – I saw her as a very harassed woman with a small child. It was significant that it happened on that particular day.

I haven't actually encountered violence myself, but I am very aware of racism in the ways people use language. Sometimes people think I am Indian and I immediately recognise the prejudice and the assumptions behind what is being said. A few days ago I phoned a student and arranged to meet him. I had not met him before. When we did, he mentioned that he just knew I was 'coloured'. I was surprised and didn't say anything at the time, but when it came up again later I asked whether he thought he could recognise the colour of my skin over the phone. Of course, I know what he meant – it was to do with my accent and his stereotype being confirmed when he met me. Again, this didn't affect me really, maybe because of the power structures involved in that situation – he was the student and I was the tutor.

I don't know at this point in time whether or not the Women's Studies course has been a turning point in my life, but all education is about change. I am probably still confused, trying to get the general picture of the state of things, where we're at regarding feminism. I would do parts of the course again. I would like to do research and to explore other forms of writing, for example. On the Women's Studies course I felt very confident after I'd been to see my tutor. She also helped me to see that there are other options that I have relative to what I am doing now. Above all, what I learnt on the course enabled me to find out a little more about myself.

8

Sue: Treading Carefully

Sue's non-specific arts background, her sense of not knowing much feminist theory and of being the only lesbian on her Women's Studies course made her tread carefully in the first instance. On her course she developed a keen interest in making videos and feminist film theory. She decided to go on and do a PhD in the area.

Getting into Studying

I started to attend the MA in Women's Studies three years ago, part-time, over two years. It was a follow-on: most of my study had been part-time. I didn't have a degree. I'm a teacher who went to a teacher training college. My main subject at college was Drama. I wasn't that wild about teaching, so I did some other things and then came back to teaching. I taught for a while and then decided that I wanted to try and get a degree, so I went to the Open University. I did my degree through the Open University. It was an arts-based one but it also introduced me to Sociology and Philosophy. By the time I finished it I'd really got into studying and when I stopped there was quite a gap. So I went to the local polytechnic (it's since become a university) to do a Philosophy evening course and got chatting to someone who knew of their Women's Studies course and it sounded really good.

Before I was told about it I had never heard of Women's Studies. I knew about consciousness-raising groups and things like that, but I hadn't thought of it in academic terms. I also did not think of myself as a feminist. I had an interest in women's issues, that was the 'nature' of my feminism, but I have a very different perspective now.

Joining the MA in Women's Studies

When I did the interview for the Women's Studies course, I was interviewed with another prospective candidate who seemed amazingly knowledgeable about feminist theory, which made me think, 'What am I doing here?' I knew nothing about feminist theory apart from the little bit that I'd picked up on one of the courses at the Open University where it had just been touched on. The interviewer, however, reassured me that it wasn't that important that I knew nothing about theory.

I did express quite a lot of interest in making videos and I rather liked the idea, as it was set up on the course then, of doing a group project. When I'd been at college before, I'd done something called 'Experimental Drama' – this was a new option on the Drama course which meant you could offer original creative practical work instead of a written dissertation. It involved working in groups, which was great. I had really enjoyed doing that and thought that the video project sounded slightly similar. As it turned out, although lots of people were very interested in doing video projects, when it came down to it I was on my own, which, in a sense, defeated why I'd come on the course.

Other People on the Course

I had no idea what sort of people would be on the course and I had no particular expectations. That openness was a good thing. The other people on the course were very interesting. Coming from an Open University background, I was used to meeting all kinds of different people. A lot of them had families or were concerned with other things.

When I first met the other people on the course I was not very confident and up to a point I went on the course to improve my confidence. To a certain extent I wanted to gain more confidence in myself, though, having said that, I should emphasise that I like myself and am not that unconfident. But from an academic point of view I wanted to gain confidence. Coming from a background of the Open University where you spend an awful lot of time on your own and talking to the walls to get your ideas flowing, only going to the occasional seminar and summer schools, it made a lot of difference being in a regular seminar with other people every week. In fact, I found that a bit overpowering, and I didn't say very much. It was in the pub afterwards that I got to know people. But in the context of the actual discussion group, I did not respond very well and I don't think I made the most of it because I was so unsure.

A lot of people who were there said they came from a definite academic discipline such as Literature or Sociology. That meant that sometimes they'd say things like, 'I don't think I can comment on this because, coming from the discipline I do, I don't know much about this,' but the other side of that coin was that they'd be very confident about something else precisely because it related directly to 'their discipline'. I did not have a definite discipline and had dabbled in lots of things. That was very useful in that I could pick up on many different discussions, but I would also feel that I had no proper academic roots.

Some of the sessions on the course I didn't relate to all that much. We seemed to go on an awful lot about being a mother, for example, and I am not one of course. Other women would talk about that endlessly. That apart, I found most topics interested me in at least some measure.

Issues of Sexual Identity

I didn't come out on the course as a lesbian until halfway through the first year. It wasn't immediate because I was sussing people out first, I guess. I felt a bit overpowered, if I'm honest – I was the only lesbian in that particular year, certainly the only one that came out. I felt that people were looking at me furtively, expecting me to make some profound statement whenever the notion of lesbianism came up and I didn't really feel that I could make such a statement. I was only talking from MY experience, after all.

At the end of the course someone said that sexuality and sexual identity should have been much more of an issue on the course. Yet there were moments when it did come up and it was almost smothered and pushed out. It was almost as if people wanted it to be an issue but it never really got developed. I did not try to be someone to bring the issue out on the course, because until the end of the course I was still building up my own confidence. Perhaps if there'd been somebody else with whom I could have bounced such ideas around, I would have done. We had one guy on the course who, like I might have been the token lesbian, was the token male. That makes things very difficult.

Doing the course made me rethink my position as a lesbian. The course in a sense politicised me. I want to carry on now and develop some of my ideas further through doing research. I didn't realise that there was so much lesbian material around. I'd become very closed in. When I first came out I was in London, I was much younger, I went in for clubbing, etc. Then I moved to Cambridge and met my partner, who likes to be out only to close friends. So we became involved with a very small personal circle of friends, none of whom were gay. Going on the course meant starting to read about being gay. That changed things for me. This hasn't affected the way my partner and I live together, but it's altered me in that I've become more independent. I used to stay at home a lot, but now I go out much more.

At the beginning of the course people were a bit worried about how to integrate personal and academic concerns. Some were worried that if you took the 'personal' aspect too far the course wouldn't be considered academic, and there was quite a strong lobby who favoured a very academically oriented course. All that changed as we got to know each other better and trust each other more. People were very wary of bringing in personal experiences as part of their argument to begin with. I wasn't sure what I thought. The various positions were all very new to me. There was one group who said that we should bring more of our stories into the course and not be so 'objective'. I think I was stuck in the middle between those who felt uncomfortable with revealing lots about themselves and others who wanted to connect their work more with their lives. But the notion that the course should be academic was always strongly present.

Moving into Research: Making the Video

I was very impressed with the writings of Judith Butler, texts on gender as performance. I was also interested in feminist writings on film theory. I had been interested in film theory before but not specifically from a feminist angle. My research started off with the notion of challenging Lacan's ideas of how identity is tied into language. That really irritated me. I did not agree with it. One of our tutors was really into psychoanalysis and it was a big thing on the course. I didn't have my arguments together enough at the time so I did not really challenge what the tutor was saying; she delivered her paper really well. But it got me thinking and issues from that came into the video that I did, the idea of the unconscious and the subconscious. I think of the unconscious as a potential narrative, and I rejected the whole idea of the Oedipal episode. I've just been reading Margaret Whitford's book on Luce Irigaray, and I think there's lots of interesting material in there. It seems that she talks of the imaginary as being an effect, produced in a kind of hermeneutic circle. It was this that I was working on in my dissertation.

As part of my dissertation I made a video. My video had started out as a poem years ago; then I made it into a short story. It seemed to me that there was the basis of a video in the two – the idea behind it just grew. The central idea was associated with the problem that women were supposed to have in the early feminist film theory around the gaze, that is their having been positioned as object, something to be looked at, rather than as subject, as lookers or viewers. In the 1970s, feminist film theory was very useful in displaying how Lacanian psychoanalytical discourse seemingly entrapped women into a non-subject position. Women were constructed as 'the other' by 'the male gaze'. Highlighting this apparently closed position of women, which allowed only objectification, led to attempts to construct ways of not repeating this positioning, that is to say to address the spectator as female rather than male.

It seemed to me that the first attempts to do this in feminist film production were through the avant-garde. Avant-garde film-making has seemingly worked in opposition to populist film, often trying to subvert its methods, particularly techniques such as shot/countershot, to draw the viewer into the narrative. This prompted some avant-garde film-makers to try to avoid narratives which allowed easy identification and to try to shift attention to the material processes of film, to try to give the spectator a position which would affirm their own reality. Narratives were regarded as authoritarian because in a way they repressed the reality of space and time. Yet it could be argued that this 'repression of reality' is needed and is part of our own internalised narratives, which continually run with us and cannot be split apart from the body's location in time and space. Narratives always exist. They may be internalised and seemingly chaotic, for time is not restricted to space when functioning internally, but they are always there potentially. This is why I feel that 'the potential for narrative' is perhaps the closest definition I could give for the term 'the unconscious'.

I wanted to make a video which used a narrative but which also highlighted the technical system of representation I was using. I have to be honest and say that this position was not completely dictated by the theories I had been reading, but was partly determined by my own personal insecurities with regard to the technical equipment I was using and the fact that I was not at all sure I could turn my written text into a film. So with the exceptions of the shots with 'Time', who was the only character played by a person, the whole process was like a dialogue between myself and the camera. This seemed to be a working through of the 'who speaks?', 'who looks?' problem, for I became the narrator and the spectator, and my original text was reformulated as I worked on it.

I addressed gender and narrative through representations which did not use 'real' visible actors but overtly displayed the power of the technical means to represent. The camera functioned as a narrator. The male character in the story is represented by the use of a mannequin. As it is a private detective it is introduced by a 'Chandleresque'-style voice-over which was supposed to build up a certain visual expectation. This was not met by the eventual sight of the supposed owner of the voice, a copy of 'reality', who then goes on in its 'own' voice to explain how fantasy helps it to feel real. I should perhaps point out that I had been working with Judith Butler's ideas and, as I understood her, she had referred to the psychoanalytic notion of gender identification as being constituted 'by a fantasy of a fantasy'.

The other main character in the video is a crab, which is constructed by an animated process using a computer and is therefore another subject in the narrative whose identity is constructed by the technical system of representation it is performing within. The crab is supposed to be the 'imaginary' for both the other characters.

As I tried to explain in the text which went with my video, I wanted to bring in the term 'imaginary' as a reference to the Lacanian discourse which I wished to question. Earlier I said that I see 'the unconscious' as a 'potential narrative', as the unused or dormant 'effects' of the body's performance in time and space which is part of the psychological core. These effects may express themselves as fantasies or desires, and can be articulated back into discourse via other performed narratives. For me the imaginary is the part of the psychological core where fantasy narratives are formulated and mixed with the narratives which the body performs. If, to follow Butler's line of argument, the gendered body is performative and has no ontological status apart from the acts which constitute its reality, then it is these acts or desires which produce the effect of an internal core. The imaginary is then an 'effect', not a 'cause'. There is no psychological core that follows the same pattern in each female or male. Each subject moves in its own particular time and space. This localisation allows for many differences of fantasy and desire to develop. There is no Oedipal moment. The imaginary is not something one moves from in a Lacanian sense. The 'psychological core' is in constant dialectic with time and place, and the discourses which inform it.

The other character in the video is the concept of 'Time'. As I said, it is the only character played by a real person, performing in front of the camera. It had to be played by a male actor as time, as we think of it, is such an androcentric concept. Also, time especially is something that is very important in our lives, so much is built around it, and yet we do not understand it very well.

I suppose one could say that the house which the camera/narrator/female character lives in is also a 'character' in the video. The idea is that the house functions as a paradigm for patriarchy, a structure which you don't even notice until you start to break it down. The narrator lives within it, unaware of its power until the crab appears and begins to question its power. The crab leaves the house and the house, fearing the crab's power, employs a private detective to try to find it. The private detective realises that the house needs the crab's affirmation of his existence and therefore refuses to collude with the house (I might be too hopeful here!). The narrator escapes to find the crab and begin to live or perform those fantasies which are meaningful to her. This destroys the house. However, it is implied that the house will be rebuilt with added Victorian features – for realism's sake! This whole scenario has the bubbling assistance of Time who, despite his seemingly powerful position, constantly questions his own identity.

The narrator drives off in a car, with Time and the crab on the back seat. Time says, 'Where to now?' and the girl replies, 'I don't know.' The film finishes with this idea of an uncertain future, but it's not a drive-off like in *Thelma and Louise* where the characters kill themselves. It's simply open-ended.

Beyond the MA in Women's Studies: A PhD

The MA in Women's Studies made me want to pursue issues about what it means for women to make films, so after finishing it I decided to do some further research. I am now looking at various women film-makers such as Lizzie Borden, Yvonne Rainer, Trinh Minh-Ha and Sally Potter. I went to see *Orlando* recently. Potter is quite an interesting film-maker. I think she's sold out in some ways. I also want to make another film myself. I hope all of this will be a PhD, the film plus a thesis.

I am trying to combine being a full-time teacher with doing research. That means that I have to do my research during holidays, because it's pretty difficult during term time. I am doing the research primarily out of a personal interest I have in the area, but if I get a chance to move into Adult Education as a result of doing the PhD, then that'll be great. I enjoy teaching at all levels in fact, and have taught at infant, primary, middle school, secondary levels. I am quite open in terms of where I go. I am not doing this research in order to change my career. But if I get my ideas together enough I'd quite like to publish something and establish some dialogue with other people working in the area.

I did not expect this to happen or that I'd want to do these things. At the end of my first degree I knew that I wanted to go on and do something, so in a way it did not surprise me when I got to the end of my MA and asked myself, 'Now what?'

Working with Others

I like to be creative, not necessarily in an academic way as such, but the chance of going on to make videos, that is important. I thought about doing a course on film and I actually started to write a film script, which has been quite useful in terms of getting me to think about what I might do. Initially I worked on a script because a friend of mine was keen to collaborate, but halfway through she dropped out. That was a familiar scenario.

When I did the MA I also wanted to collaborate with someone, but it didn't work out. In that particular year nobody seemed to be very clear about what was meant by a 'video'. People kept coming back to the idea of a 'documentary', documenting things on video. I'd never seen it like that. Other students got put off by the technical aspects of making a video. They had never been in an editing suite before, for example, had never used a camera, and whereas I wanted to learn about all of this, others seemed to feel quite threatened by it. Many people were very keen on the idea of the video, but when it came down to it they backed off. We did not have much technical tuition. I think we could have done with a lot more to help us become more proficient in dealing with the technical aspects of making the video. Also, there was the fact that you had to write as well; you couldn't *just* make a video, you had to produce written work alongside it.

At the end of the day, I suppose it came down to confidence. People who really, really wanted the MA didn't want to jeopardise the chance of getting the MA because of technical failures with the video or something like that. I was not that bothered about the MA; it didn't matter that much whether or not I got the degree. So for me it was much more about the experience of making a video.

I did try and co-opt people to collaborate for my video. When I told them about my idea about the crab, they'd back away and it just didn't work. One other person started to make a video, but she eventually just dropped out of the course completely. In the end I was the only one in my year who made a video.

I think in an odd sort of way the fact that I did make the video helped subsequent years of students. Making a practice video was really useful. All we were supposed to do was interview a person and edit it down to two minutes. This opened up lots of questions about what am I doing with what that person has said, editing it down and so on. I did not want to cut what the interviewee had said but I also wanted to learn how to use all the equipment, so I constructed a 20-minute video which allowed the interviewee to speak but also allowed me to raise the question: who speaks? Is it the person being filmed? Or the editor? Or is it the viewer? I showed this video to the following intake of students. I think it helped them that I had done the video, having no prior experience. I explained this to them and I think that gave people confidence.

I am still in contact with people who were on the course with me. Some of us live quite close to each other, and we still meet regularly. Informally, we were quite supportive of each other on the course. We used to meet in the pub afterwards and discuss issues to do with the course as well as other things.

Up to a point, of course, one wants to change things; that's what Women's Studies should do, promoting women's perspectives within academe. You've just got to walk a fine line because you have to maintain some sort of academic street cred, and it is really difficult to try and alter things without going too far – in which case nobody will listen, and the whole point is that you want people to listen to what you're saying. So you can't afford to alienate them too much.

9

Ruth: Female Friendship

Ruth, a married woman with daughters, was an undergraduate in the heyday of the Women's Liberation Movement in the late '60s and early '70s but, perhaps due to her involvement in the church, missed out on it. The desire to get out of the rut she was in encouraged her to join a Women's Studies course, which then led to her rethinking her relationships with other women and to writing a dissertation about an aunt of hers and that aunt's female friend.

Out of the Rut

I heard about the MA in Women's Studies on the radio. It wasn't clear to me that it was an MA; I just heard Women's Studies and thought that sounded interesting. I was looking for something – I didn't know what exactly I was looking for – to get out of the rut I was in. I'd had a job in a school outside of town, my first real job away from the family for twelve years, and then I lost it because I couldn't go full-time and I ended up teaching in my daughter's school. Suddenly it all became really claustrophobic again, family and all that. Everybody at my daughter's school knew me as somebody's mum or somebody's wife, and I thought, I must get out of this, but I couldn't really see a way out of it because, after all, you get paid for what you are trained for and I was trained to be a teacher. Then I heard about this course and I thought it might offer me a way forward, some ideas.

I rang the college to ask about the MA and got some information. Initially, I thought the course might be too academic for me; I wasn't sure I wanted to do anything very academic as I'd been out of education since my marriage 20 years before and I hadn't used all my previous academic work. I wanted to go on a course that I could understand and where things would be relevant to me. I think I also had some sort of idea of togetherness, which was a bit vague. I would have done the course if it hadn't been an MA. I hadn't thought about doing an MA as such before; when I found out I thought it was a bonus. After I left university when I'd done my BA, I got married and we moved and there wasn't anywhere near us where I could have done a postgraduate degree, but I would have liked to have done it then. In retrospect I am glad I didn't because I would not have done Women's Studies if I had – I would have done one of the traditional subjects, which is all that was on offer at the time. It would have been similar to what I'd done as an undergraduate where you read a textbook, went to the lecture, wrote an essay every fortnight, and finally did your exams. That was what History at Sheffield University was like.

Not a Feminist but Aware of Difference

Although I was a student in the late '60s and early '70s, I never heard of feminism, never, and I was not involved in the feminist movement at all. I never really thought about it very much until I came on the Women's Studies course. I didn't think of myself as a feminist when I began the course, but I became aware of certain things in relation to my own and other women's situation, such as being stuck at home and not having the same sort of freedom and options that men have. And men viewing life differently from women. When I was on the course I read somewhere that men tend to compartmentalise things, and I thought, 'Oh, great, it isn't just me who thinks that.' Men have little boxes and they put you in one and that's it really. When they need to, they open that box; otherwise, it's closed.

I don't know why I never heard about the Women's Movement and feminism. Now I know what I know it seems amazing, really. I had a very sheltered, a very closeted childhood and upbringing, I suppose. When I was at university I was very involved in the church most of the time I was there and afterwards; maybe it's something to do with that. Most of my life was geared around the church and feminism just wasn't an issue, certainly not in the church. In the setup I was in women were really supposed to be terribly subordinated to their husbands but that was an absolute joke – all the women who said the loudest, 'Oh, my husband's in charge' were the bossiest wives, with husbands running around after them and the women ruling the roost.

I had a brother who was to a certain extent treated differently from me, but then he was the youngest. My father took a lot of interest in him as he began to grow up and started taking him out, which he never did with us girls. But then my parents were very keen for me to go to university and for me to fulfil my potential, so I didn't have to fight for anything like that.

Falling from Grace at School

I hated my last year at school, I'm not sure why. I always had a weight problem, I was fat as a child, but I also always felt outside of things as far as other girls were concerned. I had one or two friends. But I didn't feel that I fitted somehow. And I didn't fit in the school hierarchy. When I was in the Lower Sixth, I was one of the apples of the eye of the headmistress; I was one of the first girls that she gave extra duties to. She put me in charge one day of a class of 15-year-olds because she hadn't got a teacher – this wouldn't happen today. This class was notorious, and she said, 'If you have any trouble, come and fetch me.' It was terrible. They were swearing and messing around. I just couldn't control them at all, I was only two years older than they were, so in the end I went and fetched the headmistress.

And that was it. I was never accepted again. I never got any further. I never became a prefect. And when I went to university, my prof told me – years later – that they'd interviewed me as a borderline case because of something the headmistress had put in my reference.

After that event with the class everything seemed to fall apart. Socially things fell apart. Looking back, I realise that I never connected the two things before, or at the time. But sometime during that period I was quite ill – well, not exactly, but I couldn't sleep and I went to the doctor and he put me on tranquillisers for about six months. I was only 16, 17. And I was obviously in a hell of a state. I think it was quite difficult for me at the time to articulate what I thought was going on, but I could feel that things were going on and until the Women's Studies course the school was my last experience of a woman in charge. I remember reading *Frost in May* on the course and finding other women saying that their school experience was like that.

I loved being at university. When I was 15 I decided that I enjoyed History most. I had really liked English but I liked the creative side of it, doing creative writing, and of course you lose that as you progress towards 'A' level, there is no avenue for that as all you do is English Literature. We did Shakespeare but nothing modern. The boys down the road at the boys' school did D.H. Lawrence, so we used to pour over their books and read all the naughty bits.

Women in Women's Studies

Coming on the Women's Studies course was exciting. I was 41 when I joined the course. I didn't know anybody on the course except one woman by name, so I found it exciting. It's funny but the only other thing, my children's school apart, that I've become involved in socially is the church and things have become very difficult for me there. So I'd lost a lot of confidence and had become very withdrawn, not as a person but in certain situations. But I never felt unconfident on the course, not even on the first evening, because nobody knew me. So I didn't feel daunted or put off or scared despite the fact that people said to me, 'How will you feel, going into a whole new group, not knowing anybody?' But I saw it as a way forward, as quite liberating.

I had no very clear expectation of what the people on the Women's Studies course would be like. Despite my bad experience at school, which you might expect had put me off all women, I thought that there ought to be some kind of rapport between women and I didn't get on awfully well as an equal with other women. I looked up to others in more of a mother figure sort of way, and I thought that on the course it might be possible to develop some equal relationship with other women who were similar. Looking back, I suppose I thought we might all be similar ages and that we'd all have the ability to think and to talk about and share things we were thinking about, and not just discuss nappies. It really is true that in lots of women's circles – and I found that I eventually had to stop going – you end up talking about toilet training every morning. That is what women become, quite unnecessarily.

Initially I thought we'd gel very much as a group and we'd be able to share, not necessarily intimate things, but share quite a lot personally. I imagined that there would be support and that we'd want to spend time together. I sussed out very quickly that it wasn't going to be like that. And then I decided that I would go for it for me, for whatever it was going to bring; I wasn't going to get hung up on the course. People fell into different categories: there were some people who wanted to get to know each other and spend some time together, there were others who were really interested in the work and wanted to get into that, and some people were only there to do an MA, and it took a while to sort out who wanted what.

Things weren't necessarily smooth in the study groups we had, for example. If I started again now I'd be different with the other people on the course. For one thing, I'd realistically know to start with that people had come with all these different expectations, and I would realise that you always get some real stirrers and you have to spot them pretty quickly. One of the women in my study group was a real stirrer and she caused a lot of trouble. I got on all right with her but she caused a lot of trouble in the group. She was not the only one in the group as a whole. Maybe that sort of thing has to do with lack of confidence. You'd get things like confidential talking, which really meant talking about others behind their back. People also did not always put the effort in it took to make things work. Some would never socialise, even if you invited them. There comes a point when you have to say, 'OK, if that's what you want, so be it.' There's no point in losing a lot of sleep over it.

People have this thing about losing their confidence. Some women on the course felt disempowered, felt that they could never say anything, but I never had that, which, given how I'd been in other settings prior to coming on the course, is quite surprising. But I didn't feel that in the group, that I couldn't say what I wanted to say. I wanted to be in an environment where I wasn't known and I found that on the course and found it liberating. If you come from a situation where you feel very safe or very happy, then some of the ideas in Women's Studies are really going to rock you if you accept them. Or you could look at the ideas and say, 'Yes, this is really true.' I was already in that situation. It's not as if the course gave me a completely new view. It opened up ideas for me, but I had already looked at some of these issues before and I had identified areas where I'd already said, 'Something isn't right here and here and here.' So I was prepared to look at issues such as heteropatriarchy and its influence on women's lives. The question is always: do you feel capable of accommodating change?

I found the coursework hard work but not difficult. I've always liked writing, so I didn't mind doing essays, for example. As soon as I got back into that I realised how much I'd missed it. Some of the reading was difficult, because intellectually I hadn't been challenged for a while. It wasn't just the work, it was the skills that we acquired, such as how to trace sources in the library etc., which I really enjoyed, and I want to continue to use these skills now. I found that part really exciting, working my way through library catalogues, going to specialist libraries in London, understanding how to use the CD ROM.

One of the students on our course didn't believe in sharing what marks we'd got in our essays because she thought that fostered competition. On one occasion, coming out of a tutorial, another student asked me what mark I'd got and because she kept badgering me and I couldn't actually see any reason why I shouldn't tell her, I eventually did, and the first student was absolutely furious with me. She wouldn't speak to me for about three weeks. She really was quite off with me, and for a couple of weeks I felt very unsteady. She had a way of making you feel very excluded, and for a bit I found it difficult to walk into the seminar room, and it was only because of that. Then I thought, 'This is ridiculous, I'm just not going to let that get to me – if that's her position, that's her position.' Deciding this was quite a big step for me to come to because in the past that sort of thing would have made me fade out for much longer. I don't know how conscious this was, but I realise that I went through a learning process during that phase. The student I was talking about was very powerful somehow; at one of the Christmas parties she just said, 'Well, we're not going to dance, are we?' so we all just sat there and none of us danced. It was never mentioned afterwards; only very recently some of us talked about how strange it all was.

If it happened now, I would be completely different, I wouldn't allow someone else to rule my decisions like that. Looking back, though, I think it was quite a useful experience for me personally because I came through it and I can look at it now and see it in a different light. I changed. I was very wary subsequently and that was lucky in relation to another student. We had a lot in common and she was very perceptive. She came around to my house quite a few times and told me a lot about herself before I told her anything. But this student wasn't liked much by the others because she was quite divisive in a way. She had one interesting effect on our group in that she really was into touching people and her doing it all the time made everyone else become more physically expressive with each other. This student was terribly hung up on the course and stirred a lot, but she did not leave or anything. Gradually she just faded out; she seemed to be whizzing through space, from one thing and one person to another. There was a lot of talk on the course, about the course – but that is in the nature of human interaction.

Making Friends

In the end I made some very good friends. In the first year we used to sit in the car park; eventually somebody said, 'Let's go and have a drink.' We'd always ask other people but not many of them would join in.

When we did the module on sexuality it had quite an impact on me. It was the module I found most difficult to cope with. It raised all kinds of questions for me and, on top of that, things weren't easy for me in my personal life at the time. The combination of the two really got me quite upset once or twice, and we'd go off and be talking about it and things just started to come out; we'd be talking in depth about the things that had been said in the seminar during the evening and I'd say things, or one of the others would. So we started to talk about personal experiences. We'd been quite friendly before, had gone around to each other's places once or twice, but we had only made a beginning – what friendship there was, was fairly vague. Gradually we came to share more about each other, and although the friendship didn't run entirely smoothly, especially during the Christmas period when everybody was tired and run down, we eventually settled into going out for drinks together – it just became an accepted fact.

We've become very supportive of each other. At the same time, you can end up feeding off each other's problems, becoming hysterical together over what happens in each of our lives. I did think about that for a while – but it's not been like that. Because I have done work on friendship, and I know of the danger of women sharing their pain and just sharing that and therefore becoming stuck in it, I can guard against that. We now find, I think, that we can be ourselves with each other and can say what we feel and think. That has to do with confidence.

Facing Changes

When I started on the course I didn't understand half the words that were being used, such as androcentrism and phallogocentrism, and felt completely seized up and very challenged. For the first few weeks I didn't say a lot because I didn't think I understood enough. Then I realised that I was beginning to get hold of the ideas on offer; I began to recognise words and ideas, started putting them together. So I thought, 'I've actually got as much to say as everybody else,' and that did a lot for me in terms of giving me confidence. It expanded my horizons. I started to face the idea of change, and began to look at things I'd looked at the same way for years and years in a different light. There were certain things which I read that I instantly identified with, such as the idea I mentioned before of men compartmentalising things and women seeing everything in a much more complete way. Women draw everything into one whole, and I always thought that this was my own personal problem. On the course I realised that this was not just my particular perception. That makes a difference to how you see life, because suddenly you're not just an individual victim any more; you're a woman with the same problem other women experience, and you can therefore develop the ability to look at and cope with this problem, challenge it. You may not be able to change the situation, because such change might involve other people, but you can change the way you look at these problems, and your ability to cope with them.

This changed how I act. I am much more assertive at home. Because I'd married very young, for a long time I took all my husband's values on board and had gone along with what he said. Gradually I changed. In the past I always tended to back away if there was an argument, because I thought I could never win, I'd always be outargued in the end. Now I don't do that any more. I think that's made life much more interesting, for myself as well as for my family, because I have become a more interesting person. I am sure there are people who wish that this change hadn't happened; my husband never says so, and he has been very supportive in relation to me getting the coursework done, but I'm sure he wishes I hadn't changed.

The course has helped me to look at personal things, such as a past relationship I had with a woman; it helped me to bring it out and look at it again. That is not to say that the course has resolved everything for me, but it made me look at the whole question of my sexual identity, for example. I didn't realise it at the beginning, but as the course progressed I began to see that I'd chosen it because certain aspects of the course were very relevant to me; the course did find echoes in me, it related to issues in myself I wanted to deal with. I was to some extent aware of that at the beginning of the course, but somehow you don't consciously choose a course for that reason.

A Position of Relativism

There is always the whole question of labelling. While I was writing my dissertation, which was about female friendship, and brought up the issue of labels, of whether women are friends, lovers, lesbians or what, I didn't really think about it all in relation to myself. But on reflection it's interesting that I found women's friendship difficult in the past, and on the Women's Studies course I found women's friendship very significant. That may have been one reason why I decided on my dissertation topic. It went along hand in hand with the development of the friendships on the course. I couldn't consciously connect the two together but they are related. Then there's the whole sexual part of it: am I a lesbian, am I not?; obviously I'm not completely; was I in the past while I had the friendship with that woman?; does it matter anyway?

Now I don't feel threatened by that. I've decided that this is me and sometimes I relate to people in certain ways. That may sound very complicated, but I'd rather accept the complications. I think I've come from a background where everything's very black and white, and you're this or you're that, and this is right and that is wrong. And I've stepped back from that now and I'm saying, 'I don't know, I don't know.' I am not sure at all about what's right and what's wrong, what's grey. And I'm not hung up about it any more. I've acquired a position of relativism. That does add complications because my husband isn't like that, not really. I'm aware of that even if he may not argue it out. He still wishes that I was like I was a few years ago when I was like that too and I was somebody he could contain. I am not any more.

Other people apart from my husband think I've changed too, like this woman who's a friend of mine. I said to her, 'I don't need anybody the way that I used to need people.' She finds that quite hard; she said, 'It's nice to be needed.' She finds it difficult that I don't feel I need her any more for whatever reason I used to in the past. I talked to another friend of mine recently and told him that people have real problems with the fact that I've changed. He said, 'Oh, yes, you've changed.' But he likes the way I've changed; I suppose he's not in a position to feel threatened by how I've changed, although he could have done. I asked him how he thought I'd changed and he said, 'I think you've become who you are, the person you really are.' I found that very interesting, especially coming from a man. He was aware of some potential in me that he feels somehow has become released. I was really pleased by what he said, because he had accepted and seen the change in me and didn't really feel threatened by it.

I am quite interested in writing a book out of my dissertation now but I would also quite like to do something more long-term. I don't want to stay in teaching. I want to continue to use my mind and mixing with other women and adults. I'm quite keen on the idea of working in publishing or with women's organisations in some way. At present I feel a bit lost. In the last two years, because of the course, I used to think, 'I ought to be reading' all the time but now I don't have that pressure, and I miss the incentive it provided. As long as I was on the course that was my work. I feel lazy now. It's terrible how quickly you get back into a sort of idle routine.

I would certainly do the course again. I really loved it, and it was terrible when the course had started again after I'd finished and I wasn't on it any more. A friend who was also on the course said to me at one point, 'You realise the course has started again,' and we both agreed that we couldn't imagine how it could continue without us.

10

Gina: The Challenge of Difference

A woman of 60, with an upper-middle-class, quasi-Victorian upbringing, a past of raising four children by herself, of being Chairwoman of the Education Committee of her local council, and an active Tory, Gina decided to do an MA in Women's Studies as a challenge to herself.

The Shaping Past

I am 60 now. My family is enormous. I had a very successful grandfather who had seven children. Two were killed in the First World War. My grandfather made a lot of money in shipping, sailing ships without insurance and such. He became very rich and very religious, giving all his money to the church, much to his grandchildren's disgust. He used to be known as Holy Joe, handing out religious tracts in the back of his boat while his partner sailed in the front. Both his daughters went to university; one qualified as a doctor in the 1890s sometime; the other was a chief magistrate in Bristol. Two uncles went to the House of Commons, and my grandfather was in the War Cabinet too; National Unionist rather than Conservative. So there were high expectations of everybody, and there was an assumption that you just did things. There was no pressure, though, to do so really, which I'm sure in part is a class thing.

My family both encouraged and discouraged education. My brothers all went to Winchester and my sister and I went to Westonbirt, a girls' boarding school. I just assumed that this was normal. Money never really negatively impinged on my parents, though they realised that with five children life wasn't going to be quite that straightforward, especially if you worked in the maintained sector. My father was a psychiatrist at the Maudsley Hospital and the Ministry of Health. He worked in the Health Service because he was wealthy enough to do so, as my grandfather had made enough money so that he didn't need to work for a living, so to speak; he had a private income. There were quite a few missionaries and a lot of travel in my family.

I left school at 17 because I wasn't doing very well – I don't know why – and I suppose my parents were rather relieved not to have to pay the fees any longer. So I went first to a Domestic Science college and then to Art school, which is what I wanted to do anyway, and then I got married and was expected to live happily ever after. This followed very much an expected pattern. It was certainly a world where my brothers were expected to get the jobs and I was expected to get married and have children. I always think I was one of the last of a generation, the last year almost of women who were not expected to get jobs. All my contemporaries became secretaries before they got married and when they got married they didn't work again. That was basically the pattern. After that women were beginning to get jobs, but in my world they didn't at all. At the time I did not expect to deviate from that pattern. I was a bit irritated when my father, on my brother becoming a doctor, gave him a car; I said, 'I passed my exams, why can't I get a car?' and was told, 'Well, it's not the same.' There was that sort of attitude, but not excessively so. We were happy.

Just like the 1870s

I got married at 21, which seems amazing now. I have talked to my aunts, and really it was rather like the 1870s, my experience: the only way to get away from home was to get married. It was just the norm. It may be that I got married just a little bit sooner than everybody else. We lived in London for three years and enjoyed life, then came up to Northampton, of which I didn't even know where it was – nobody knew where it was. It might as well have been in Scotland. The motorway hadn't been built and it could have been anywhere.

Soon after I arrived in Northampton, I had twins. I'd just applied for one of these Churchill scholarships to go to America and travel around there a bit, because I was just beginning to think that I would like to do something – but I had twins instead. Then I developed into doing exactly what we had all been brought up to do – voluntary work. I was in the Girl Guides for 20 years; I wanted to be a magistrate but that didn't work out; eventually in 1967 I became a county councillor, doing it in a very *ad hoc* way while collecting children from school, so I never finished a meeting, and just enjoying it. But then it was very nearly a leisure pursuit in those days; it wasn't political. You appointed a Chairman or Chairwoman who was the best person for the job. It was, of course, a preselected world so you were selecting from those who had been preselected already, though you didn't realise that. The quarterly county council meeting used to start at 10.30 in the morning; by 11.30 we were all finished, we chatted till 12 and then the men used to go off to their club and have lunch. It was just a rubber stamp: nobody argued, nobody discussed anything; all the landed gentry were represented on the council, and there were Independents, Liberals. Ladies were expected to wear hats and I did, once or twice. At the time I never thought much about it, mainly because I was too busy at home. I can remember the first time I went to a meeting I drove off from home and thought, 'Gosh, this is the first time I have been me in five years.' I can remember that exhilaration very clearly. Being me meant not looking after everybody else, having to think, not just to do or manage.

I think all the time what I've done is challenged things a bit, though not much, not waving flags or anything, but I was and am known for my awareness about inequalities. The men at the council meetings used to go to the men's club at lunchtime, and I was expected to go off and do the family shopping during the lunch hour. There's an old boys' network that's still in operation, and patronage was very strong. You were aware of it being done to you: people would say things like, 'We'd better have her because she's been around a long time.' Now ability is more important and people are allowed to speak up much more. In those days you didn't really.

Women's Studies: A Real Challenge

On and off during the last five years I've thought I'm in a complete rut; the children have grown up, they've all been to university and I thought that I could basically do with a challenge. Women's Studies was an area I was interested in; in the '70s people would say to me, 'God, I hope she doesn't mention women's lib again.' I was quite aggressive about women being allowed to be equal, I suppose. I did always have the caveat that at least single women ought to be allowed to be equal, because at least they didn't have any home responsibilities so why shouldn't they be equal? That was about the level of my feminism. I have always wanted to understand what the role of women was.

Why do Women's Studies now? Well, I looked at the course two years ago and it seemed very interesting. I thought I'd like to know more about it, and do it. I didn't quite appreciate the rigour of the course, what would be involved academically. But it seemed to me a real challenge. I suppose at the back of my mind there was also this thing that if the children can get degrees, why shouldn't I?

I wasn't sure what the course would be like, though I got an inkling when I was interviewed. I hoped it would help me clarify my thoughts about women and the future; I am less interested in the past than in the future. I thought I'd be looking at things in a different light. I already in a sense have challenges in my life in that I have two daughters-in-law, one who works and one who doesn't, and I really want, in some way, to try and see the future way forward for women; how you manage your life and children. One of my concerns is that nobody seems to bother about the children at the moment. They're all so busy with their own lives that their children do not get the time and support they need. I have worked with the social services as much as education; all the children that come up for care who've been subject to major abuse have had no love, no attention, no support from their parents. They can't get over that. Even in a children's home with 30 children they sometimes get more attention than they had at home. Now this may apply across society at all times anyway, and perhaps it's to do with the class structures and issues of poverty. The fact that feminists are challenging everything but, it seems to me, not offering many positive solutions or ways forward, is what interests me here. Feminists challenge patriarchy but they don't seem to offer many solutions for the future. There should be things such as 'parental leave' for both sexes, for example.

The challenge which I expected from Women's Studies was in part to do with the fact that it was a degree course and in part to do with it being Women's Studies. I thought I'd be meeting a whole range of people that I don't normally meet, and I would like to be able to understand how they work. But the women on the course weren't as different as I expected. I thought they'd come from a range of backgrounds, they'd be more feminist and more left-wing, and more lesbian – a lesbian, left-wing hornets' nest – and I thought I'd be the catalyst for lots of lively debate, being so different. I expected it to be very, very interesting. In my view I was in a rut and I'd been in the same world for too long.

The other people on the course turned out to be nurses and women in similar jobs who appeared simply to want a further qualification. In fact, I think in my year the course was rather dominated by health professionals. There's nothing wrong with that, but they saw the course very much as a step in their career and in fact I don't know why some of them did Women's Studies as against any other qualification at all. This may be because they are at different points in their career from myself, still wanting to progress. And I don't disagree with that attitude. It is very much about professional development. All nurses will soon have to have a degree and these women are getting one step ahead, which seems logical enough.

In any event, I suppose that as you get to know people what you find out is that they all have personal as well as other reasons for coming on the course. They've all been subject to abuse of some sort or they're mentally battered by men or by their families. That is true of myself to a degree. My first husband always assumed he was in control: I managed and he led. When there was a holiday he'd say, 'Well, shall we go to x?' and then just went ahead with that. There was not much consultation. This got just worse and worse. I wanted to be in an equal partnership but it certainly was not equal. It became an unacceptable life. Once I divorced him, I was very short of money providing for four children, so I got frustrated. I saw all my friends succeeding, and going on in their careers etc. as couples, and I was moving in the opposite direction so I was slightly angry about that.

Everybody on the Women's Studies course has, I think, a personal as well as a professional agenda. Maybe that's why there are so many mature women on the course. In our group I would say there is a sort of suppressed anger, anger in a whole range of ways. As a result there's an enormous pleasure in being able to say anything you like, in fact the sorts of things you'd never say anywhere else. It takes time to realise that other women have had similar experiences to yourself; but the problem is, there's so little time on the course to get to know anyone well. This is a major issue – when we did a group project we found it virtually impossible to get everyone together at the same time. I feel quite jealous of people who have a whole year out to do a course like this. But doing that would be terribly selfish; with age you accumulate responsibilities and you can't just abandon these. If you cast them aside, it may be very difficult to pick them up again and you may not want to lose all these things. As I get older, I begin to feel that if you let things go, you may have problems. Other people will fill the gap you have left.

The world is changing for me. I am unlikely, in contrast to some of the other women on the course, to continue in or return to a job – I probably wouldn't apply for one now whereas once upon a time I might have done. I do think about what I might have done. But with four children I was trapped earlier on in my life in terms of looking after them, and financially any work I did would have meant that it would have been taken off their university grants, so I was in a pseudo-poverty trap. And then it was too late. So I got more involved in county council politics and with my Tory gang. I feel I have achieved quite a lot there, particularly as Chairwoman of the Education Committee with its budget of £250 million – unseen in many respects – typically the woman's lot. What I have done has (a) been interesting, (b) made my children respect me because they know there are a lot of challenges involved in politics, even at a local level, where you have to stand up and speak on all the things many people disagree with, such as the Education Bill – which was very hairy. This can be extremely unpleasant. With some of it you can say, 'Oh well, that's just politics,' but some of it got very personal and nasty.

Because I had an interest, our family life was good. We were all equal. This was one of the spinoffs of not having a husband around. I divorced when I was 40 – the boys were adolescent at the time. While being a single mother was tough, life was pretty unacceptable the other way around; he was an alcoholic, and in and out of psychiatric hospitals in the end. We all felt guilty about it, but he used to come and stay at Christmas and Easter and such. That was so that he could see the children and they could talk to him on their terms. It's like having a leg and then losing it; you either survive or you don't.

Being on my own in my middle years and bringing up the children alone affected me in various ways. I notice now I have remarried that I get invited to more dinner parties, and it is perfectly true, the prejudice about single people. Quite ridiculous really. However, as I was leading a very busy life which was also very social, being active in politics and in the local constituency, I didn't notice it too much. You could go to parties all the time even if you paid for your ticket. I also have one or two very good friends and a very large family who have always been supportive. So in the circumstances, while I was short of money, I also knew that there was always someone I could fall back on. However, I do understand poverty better as a result, though it was not extreme for me; I understand the exhaustion of it.

The Learning Experience

People also come to Women's Studies because it is interdisciplinary. You can explore lots of things. I also found the local college where I went to do the MA in Women's Studies, and where in fact I'd been a governor for many years and so have known it very well, an academically non-threatening place. It copes with people who are not highflyers and is therefore a kinder environment.

My experience of the course now is very different from what I expected. We all say that at the beginning we went through our book list and tried to read the texts and it was pretty well impossible. You didn't know where to start. But now it's not too bad. Some of it's a bit indigestible still, but halfway through the course you're beginning to make sense of it all. It's been an enjoyable learning experience. It's a great feeling for me just to go out and buy books for myself – it's a freedom that I haven't had before. Now I can go and buy books and not feel guilty, which is very exciting. You feel you've moved into a different world, which is quite challenging. Four years ago I remarried; my husband works in the academic world and has been a great help teaching me how to use a word processor, without which my essays would have been neither literate nor ever finished.

Academically the course is quite difficult. Having to think about theoretical issues is difficult. I thought it would be more practical research-oriented rather than working through academic arguments. That's the bit I find tough. I thought I could go and just do a whole lot of research on unmarried mothers, for example, just go off, find things out and put a package together. I would have enjoyed that. I could of course have done this in my coursework. One of the women on the course has always had a particular focus on coping with death; she's done a lot of work around that. Perhaps I should have gone about my work in a similar way. I have lurched around a bit.

There's been a lot of stuff on the course that I haven't come across before. I find the social sciences side hair-raisingly jargonistic, and some books on feminist theory very difficult, not so much now as when I first started the course. I am a very practical person; I like to find solutions and reasons rather than theorise. Well, reasons are about theory really. I find it difficult when tutors are overtly political or personal, and I am inclined to challenge things. I like it when we engage with and follow through with ideas, when there is some academic rigour and a structure to the sessions.

My study group on the Women's Studies course worked very well – to all our surprise, I think, because we're all very different, busy, not living in close proximity. We could never get everyone together so there were never the same people twice. For our group project we decided to look at Madonna and Marilyn as icons; having decided on that, people, because they hadn't been there for one meeting, would wonder whether it was a good topic or not. In the end we decided we had to fix on a subject. So we did. Looking at Madonna and Marilyn was like looking at something completely alien; no, not alien, alien is not the right word, though Madonna is pretty alien. She challenges a whole lot of things. All the other women in my study group were really shocked about the *Sex* book, more shocked than I was, which I found quite interesting. My daughter-in-law, who's a lawyer, was really shocked. I thought it was awful but that was all. I helped to keep the focus in the study group, I think. I usually tried to be on time and do what I had said I would, very cautiously though, because I didn't want to upset anybody. There was no friction, which was great.

Being at college is a sort of leveller, as it were. We all come from different backgrounds and go back to different contexts. I didn't come to college thinking I'd make a whole lot of new friends that would last me for the rest of my life, so for me that's OK. Some women perhaps came wanting more of a support mechanism, but most of the women have jobs so they know that they can only afford so much time for the course. I think people would like, if offered at the right time, a weekend away to get to know each other better – even if it was a sort of outward-bound weekend. I thought when I first came on the course that people would stay in college longer after the taught session had finished, have lunch and discussions together, battle with the library. But everybody disappears. If you have to make the effort there's always the question of is it worth the bother, will it make any difference, and there are always other things one might be doing. I don't even know where to go and find a room to sit in. We don't really have time to evolve into friendships.

Getting oneself organised is difficult when you're part-time. It's very easy to get distracted and to put other things before the course. I thought that over the summer I'd have a lot of time to do reading, but then there's the grass to cut and all sorts of other things, and time just goes. I don't think there's too much work on the course but I do live in a world where I am out every night, which makes it hard because you basically have to be very organised. I don't think I'd find that easier if I was full-time and living at home, because of the children and so on.

Change

I think I've changed as a result of being on the course. Other people certainly think I've gone left. I don't know that I have in a big way. All my daughters-in-law, and I've got three now, think it's great that I'm doing Women's Studies. So in an odd way it's been quite a big ego trip for me in my relation to them. It's been quite helpful in fact. I discuss some of the things I do on the course with them and they now think that I understand some of their problems in a different way, and they like the fact that I am using my brain, if nothing else. Once the children went to university I thought of them as leading their lives and that I had turned into their best friend rather than their mother. This was partly because I was on my own, which meant that there wasn't them and us. In a sense, I am not an interfering mother. I've never babysat yet – I'm not that sort of grandmother. I accept that their lives, which I don't always agree with, are theirs and it's up to them to decide their lives. I get concerned for them of course, whether they are happy or not and if things are going smoothly. But I stand back.

Growing up in my family, which was Scottish, people never showed emotions. My mother never showed any emotions at all. There were lots of cuddles and love, but you never discussed anything at all. I find it a bit easier now to talk about these things. That's the result, I think, of having to manage on your own, your own life, your own emotions and not being able to share them easily. It's emotions, perhaps, rather than sexuality, that are the difficulty. But the whole of society is freer now. There's a whole language which is used today – words like 'condom', even 'contraception' for example, which, if used at all, were whispered and which weren't in anybody's day-to-day language when I was younger – now it's open, which makes things easier.

I would like to see some discussion on women in management studies and personnel in Women's Studies because more and more women are in that situation now and they are the ones who might try to change things in society at large, at least in a work context. I would perhaps have liked to have the group project focused on and tied to a specific, larger project so that it contributed a bit to a wider research concern. Some of the group projects that were done seemed a bit pointless to me.

We haven't looked much at ageism on the course. Yet the majority of elderly people are women, and the percentage is increasing. There are many elderly widows, for example, women who'll live on their own for 20 or 30 years even, and often in reduced financial circumstances. In Women's Studies people tend to think in terms of the active feminist 30-year-old or so. That is a problem. Nobody appears to be interested in health education or pre-retirement courses. People tend to think that you are simply going downhill, which isn't the case. You should be thinking about the openings, what doors and windows are going to be open to you as a consequence of retiring. But people just tend to think you're over the hill. The likelihood is that you're going to live until you're 80 or 85. So you may have a quarter or a third of your life left after retirement. There's an assumption that as you're an adult you know everything, but I see the gaps all the time and it isn't so.

I took up Women's Studies to shift myself from where I was and to have an intellectual challenge. In the world I was in, unless you are the Chairperson you reach a certain point beyond which you can't go. Once you're off that log you can't sit around and grumble or stir. The challenges that I was hoping for did occur as a result of the course. I've learnt a lot. People keep coming up and asking about the how and where and why of the course. It's changed my own focus, and I have acquired a different status in the outside world as a result of doing the course. I hope this will encourage other women not to return to the kitchen sink when they or their husbands retire, but also to find new interests and activities.

Section III

Experience in Women's Studies

11

Experiential Authority and Heterosexuality

CELIA KITZINGER

In their book on *Women's Ways of Knowing*, Mary Belenky and her colleagues describe a male professor taking the first class of an introductory science course:

> The professor marched into the lecture hall, placed upon his desk a large jar filled with dried beans, and invited the students to guess how many beans the jar contained. After listening to an enthusiastic chorus of wildly inaccurate estimates the professor smiled a thin, dry smile, revealed the correct answer, and announced, 'You have just learned an important lesson about science. Never trust the evidence of your own senses.'...
> The lesson the science professor wanted to teach is that experience is a source of error. (Belenky *et al* 1986, pp. 191, 193)

By contrast, feminist pedagogy is supposed to consider women's experience as central, as a key source of our knowledge. 'Women have been driven mad, "gaslighted", for centuries by the refutation of *our experience* and our instincts in a culture which validates only male experience' (Rich 1975, p. 10; emphasis added); and 'a central development of "Women's Studies method" has been to incorporate *our own experiences* and perceptions as women into both teaching and research' (Coyner 1983, p. 63; emphasis added). When, as feminists, we asserted that we were the experts on our own lives, that we would no longer permit men to speak on our behalf or to give us their 'expert' views on what it means to be a women, we laid claim to the inviolability of personal experience and to the right to interpret it on our own terms. We asserted the importance of 'experiential authority'.

A decade or so later, feminists within the academy have begun to point to the serious problems of invoking experiential authority in the classroom. We have discussed the dilemmas associated with expecting (or requiring) that students expose personal experience in the context of a hierarchical academic institution, within which their progress in being assessed and monitored: 'the personal as political' can seem a threatening imperative when associated with the surveillance and scrutiny of a university degree course, and can provoke unease and possibly resistance. Many feminists (for example Humm 1991, p. 53) have also pointed out that 'our experience' as women is diverse and sometimes contradictory – a diversity often negated in general statements about 'women's experience' which falsely construct 'woman' as a single unitary category across differences of ethnicity, class and sexual identity. 'Our' experience all too often turns out to be the common and unproblematised knowledge only of white, middle-class, able-bodied, heterosexual Anglo-Americans (see Simmonds 1992; Bhavnani 1992). While acknowledging these difficulties, I want in this chapter to raise some other problems I have encountered in my own attempts to teach issues of sexual identity on a Women's Studies MA, on a 'Feminism & Psychology' module of a Social Psychology BA and in numerous invited workshops. The problems that concern me are questions about who has the 'right' to speak on the basis of 'experiential authority', what that authority enables one to say (and the limits it imposes), who is silenced by the invocation of 'experience', and the implications of all this for feminist theory.

'Speaking as a Lesbian ...'

It is unusual, in the context of Women's Studies, for lesbians to be accused of sickness and perversion, although not uncommon for complaints to be made about 'bias' and 'excessive preoccupation' with lesbian issues. The following extract from a student evaluation form completed at the end of the first term of a Women's Studies MA course gives a flavour of this problem:

> I felt that the bias of the module was towards lesbian issues. Some of the handouts were very radical indeed. I felt intimidated by the enthusiasm for alternative literature, music, and lesbian viewpoints. Lesbian issues were too much to the forefront.

My lesbian 'bias' was widely commented on by students on this course, but unlike the student quoted above, many (including heterosexual students) saw this 'bias' in very positive terms: 'great to realise that "Women's Studies" is about lesbians too'; 'it was interesting to have a lesbian perspective on these issues'; 'I particularly valued the lecturer's open and forthright way of dealing with lesbian concerns'; 'my first ever experience of dealing with lesbian issues – a struggle, but very educational'. I have generally found heterosexual students interested in and respectful of 'my experience' as a lesbian. They are concerned to demonstrate their own acceptance of lesbianism, careful to acknowledge my 'different' viewpoint, and extremely cautious in challenging any statements prefaced with the phrase 'As a lesbian, I ...'

The roles of 'teacher' and 'student' on Women's Studies courses have been theorised elsewhere (for instance France 1983; Bowles and Klein 1983) and it is not my intention to rehearse those arguments here. Whatever 'authority' I have over students by virtue of my position in the institutional hierarchy, my control over their grades and exam marks and so on, that 'authority' is enormously enhanced when I lay claim to explicit personal experience of the topic under discussion. Far from feeling 'exposed' or 'vulnerable' when describing lesbian experience in the classroom, I am aware of drawing on a resource which is actually *more convincing* and carries *more authority* for many students than does a scholarly review of the academic or feminist literatures or a detailed analysis of any one of a number of theoretical positions. The personal is tremendously powerful rhetoric within and beyond the classroom. Experiential authority is valued above 'abstract theory' not just within the Women's Studies context, but within feminism more broadly.

My experiential authority on lesbianism goes pretty much unchallenged by heterosexual students: at most, they point out that I can speak only on behalf of that subgroup of lesbians whose racial/ethnic backgrounds, (dis)ability and class status parallel my own. The same respect for experiential authority is accorded to those of the group who have children when we theorise motherhood, for example, or to those of the group who are Black, Asian or Irish when we theorise racism. In the course of such discussions, students who do not share the experiential authority that would make them 'experts' in the given context seem to be engaged in careful self-monitoring, fearful lest they say anything that might attract accusations of prejudice. They are relatively passive, absorbing expert opinions rather than critically engaging with the theories under discussion, anxious about 'invalidating' other women's realities, hesitant of expressing views which might be at variance with a 'politically correct' perspective.

This stands in stark contrast with class discussions of heterosexuality. When I address the topic of heterosexuality I make clear that (unlike many lesbians) I am discussing that of which I have no direct personal experience – no past or present heterosexual identity, activity or desire. It is evident, then, that the source of my knowledge about heterosexuality is quite different from the source of my knowledge about lesbianism. What I 'know' about lesbianism fits the Women's Studies model of being drawn from personal experience. What I 'know' about heterosexuality is 'pure theory', not rooted in 'the personal'. On the topic of heterosexuality, I lack experiential authority, and this lack of authority is evident in student responses.

Lesbian students with heterosexual pasts who share my radical lesbian feminist perspective quite often leap in with their own experiences to 'help me out', supporting my theoretical perspective on heterosexuality with the 'experiential authority' I so regrettably lack. Both heterosexual and lesbian students often challenge my analysis, drawing on their own experiential authority of pleasure in heterosexual sex, of continuing heterosexual desire or happy marriages to 'refute' my theories: 'How can you say anything about heterosexuality when you've no experience of it yourself?' 'It's all very well to be critical of heterosexuality, but you don't know how wonderful sex with a man can be'; 'I love my boyfriend – doesn't my experience count for more than your theories?' To speak as a lesbian on the topic of heterosexuality, especially to speak openly from the position of a lesbian who has never been heterosexual, is to speak without experiential authority and hence to speak without credibility.

But it is more than this; it is also to speak out of turn. Heterosexuality has of course been theorised by lesbians for a very long time (for example the Leeds Revolutionary Feminist Group 1981; Rich 1980); our recent edited collection on heterosexuality (Wilkinson and Kitzinger 1993) is less remarkable for being edited by two lesbians than it is for having 23 contributions from *heterosexual* feminists theorising their experience. Nonetheless, the intensely vivid, personal and politically engaging accounts from these heterosexual contributors have been largely overlooked in the reviews to date, in favour of attacks on our right and competence, as lesbians, to edit such a collection in the first place. In responding to such attacks we have sometimes drawn on experiential authority, pointing to one of the co-editors' extensive past heterosexual experience (including a 15-year marriage) and arguing that no lesbian, under heteropatriarchy, can be ignorant of heterosexuality and its operation, since it is everywhere blatantly flaunted and propagandised. But such arguments assume, as do the criticisms, that only experiential authority 'counts' and that without personal experience of hetero-sexuality we are debarred from speaking. The effect of such an assumption is to silence lesbians.

The price of claiming that only lesbians have the 'right' to theorise lesbianism appears to be the parallel claim that only heterosexuals have the 'right' to theorise heterosexuality. The 'private ownership' model of experience means that lesbians are relegated to theorising lesbianism (while heterosexuals are relieved of any such responsibility) and are debarred from theorising heterosexuality – which often means the prohibition of *any* thor-oughgoing critiques of heterosexuality at all, since heterosexual feminists have been understandably reluctant to problematise heterosexuality *per se*. Heterosexual women, prepared to grant lesbians expertise on the topic of lesbianism, respond with anything from indignation to outrage when we invade 'their' territory. In fact, so much do they feel that heterosexuality is their exclusive province that lesbians who theorise heterosexuality are sometimes treated as marauding invaders, selectively plundering heterosexual experience for evidence of our own superior way of life. Since editing the 'heterosexuality' book, we have learned that heterosexuality is the 'private property' of heterosexuals, and that lesbians who trespass on heterosexual terrain are viewed as having illegitimately appropriated space not rightfully theirs, taking liberties with heterosexual experience, 'speaking out of turn', even (in an extraordinary reversal) 'silencing' heterosexual women. Experiential authority, then, prevents dialogue (your have your experience, I have mine, and mine is off limits to you) and leads to the silencing of lesbians.

In sum, for many contemporary feminists, it seems, each woman speaks only of the particularities of her own life, never generalising beyond the personal, maintaining a respectful silence in the face of other women's diverse and contradictory experience.

Beyond Narcissism

The idea that only those with the appropriate experiential knowledge have the 'right' to theorise can function to reinforce a kind of narcissism, such that women fail to move beyond the confines of their own current experiences. In the Women's Studies classroom, heterosexual students seem often to feel either that lesbian concerns are 'nothing to do with them', or that, while they may have something to learn from the discussion of lesbian issues, they must do so passively, not presuming to contribute anything. What, then, is the position of heterosexual (and bisexual) students in theorising lesbianism? Are they limited to 'dealing with internalised homophobia', otherwise there simply to listen – absolved of the responsibility of contributing except for trying to deal with their own anti-lesbian feelings? Are they, lacking experiential authority of lesbian oppression, debarred from theory development?

Given the decades of (continuing) misrepresentation of lesbians in heterosexual feminist theory, we may appreciate the poetic justice of demanding that heterosexuals absent themselves from lesbian theory development, leaving the field to lesbians only. But I think we need to demand more of heterosexuals than absence, compliance and silence. Lesbian feminist theory is not and never has been 'for lesbians only' (Bunch 1975). I want heterosexual feminists actively to engage with lesbian issues, and to contribute to them. It is not enough simply to assert, as many of my students do, that 'lesbian experience is so different from my own that I would not presume to discuss it'. Heterosexual feminist theory that omits lesbian issues, or which simply tacks on lesbian concerns as developed by lesbians (and not integrated into the theory itself), is accountable for its silences, its absences. Discussing the problem of writing about 'difference' in fiction, Anna Livia (a white, gentile, able-bodied novelist) asks:

> In whose interest is it that white women should feel Black experience is so different from ours as to be unimaginable? Or that sighted women should believe the thoughts of blind women to be on such a different pattern that we will not venture to guess them? When gentile women read the work of Jewish women, it must be because we assume we will understand some, I venture to say even most, of what has been written. Probably we will not understand as much as other Jewish women, but enough to feel the book is worth our engagement … I don't think the author's personal experience is a reasonable criterion on which to judge a novel. We must take on the whole world; we cannot afford 'no go areas' of the imagination; we cannot afford to refuse an opinion on any subject. If we insist that no one may write about anyone's experience save her own, we are condemning ourselves to a literature of reporting.
>
> (Livia 1989, pp. 33–4)

When we say that heterosexual women cannot be expected to engage with lesbian concerns, we are letting them off the hook. They have not just a 'right' but an obligation actively to theorise lesbianism. As Anna Livia says, they can only get it wrong; and the costs of their getting it wrong are outweighed by the benefits of their at least attempting to engage with our lives. Trying – and running the risk of getting it wrong – may well be a frightening endeavour for heterosexual women, terrified of accusations of anti-lesbianism, but one which we must surely find ways of encouraging in the Women's Studies classroom.

The Politics of Experience

Many feminists have written of the way in which feminism in general, and Women's Studies in particular, 'can give support to women's experiences' (Humm 1991, p. 49). And often of course it does: feminist work on child sexual abuse, sexual harassment, childbirth, marital rape and in many other arenas has validated and named the experience of many women. But equally, it is also true that sometimes feminist theory actively *contradicts* individual women's experience.

Take, for example, a workshop I ran in which a lesbian student spoke with enthusiasm of the latest 'discovery' of a 'gay gene', saying that this confirmed and supported her own experience of having been 'born gay'. She was challenged by a heterosexual student who spoke of the dangers of such biological theories, their eugenicist implications, and the likelihood of most women being born potential lesbians but coerced into compulsory hetero-sexuality. The lesbian student retorted, with some passion, that in invoking such theories the heterosexual women was 'negating my experience' and 'invalidating my reality'. Had this debate occurred between two lesbians, they might have agreed to accept their differences: part of the 'charge' of this interaction was because it involved two women with different sexual identities, with the heterosexual woman presuming on lesbian territory. The effect of the lesbians student's retort was to draw attention to the other's lack of experiential authority, resulting in an embarrassed retreat by the heterosexual student. In asking students to reflect on this exchange, I directed their attention to questions such as: can a heterosexual student challenge a lesbian student's analysis of lesbianism without this automatically being labelled 'homophobia'? Is it possible, permissible, to challenge the voices of the oppressed (with anything other than the words of other oppressed groups)? And when a heterosexual student theorises lesbianism, in what ways is her process of theory development the same as, and in what ways different from, the process of theory development undertaken by a lesbian student theorising heterosexuality?

In my own teaching, it seems that students have a simple answer to these questions. In any dispute, the person who can claim the relevant experiential authority is seen as having the most right to speak, especially where she can also claim to be the most oppressed. So a lesbian theorising lesbianism is on safe ground, virtually unchallengeable by a heterosexual woman; whereas a heterosexual woman theorising lesbianism can be challenged by lesbians as lacking both experiential authority and an understanding of oppression. A lesbian theorising heterosexuality lacks experiential authority but, being (by virtue of her lesbianism) more oppressed, is imagined to speak in a 'purer', more 'authentic' voice. As such, the situations are not parallel: the lesbian speaks with more authority on heterosexuality than the heterosexual can on lesbianism, and it is this notion of lesbian purity or moral superiority that seems to render lesbian theories of heterosexuality so very threatening to heterosexual feminists – and hence leads to some of the more florid attacks on lesbian theorists. It is important, for the development of feminism, that we judge the adequacy of feminist theories in terms of their political utility, or predictive power, rather than in terms of the author's biography and her presumed 'right' (or lack of it) to create theory.

A large part of the problem lies in the term 'experience'. It is not possible, as some feminists have suggested, simply to 'discover what we know'. Experience is not logically 'prior', basic, the building block of theory, and cannot be posited as unproblematic authentic 'fact', the touchstone of reality. Experience is never 'raw': it is embedded in a social web of interpretation and reinterpretation. Women's (or lesbians') 'experience' does not spring uncontaminated from an essential inner female way of knowing, but is structured within, or in opposition to, the discourses provided by heteropatriarchy. There is no such thing as 'a-theoretical' experience. Experience is always perceived through an implicit or explicit theoretical framework within which it gains meaning. Feelings and emotions are not simply immediate, unsocialised, self-authenticating responses. They are socially constructed and presuppose certain social norms. Placing 'experience' beyond debate is deeply anti-feminist because it denies the social roots of our 'inner selves', denies the political sources of experience and renders it purely personal.

Consequently, when 'theory' apparently 'negates' someone's 'experience' it is necessary to explore the theoretical framework within which that 'experience' is already perceived and reported. As we grow up, we learn certain ways of thinking about our experience, and as feminists we learn to think about that experience in different ways. What we may have thought of, with self-hatred and guilt, as a dirty childhood game is reinterpreted as child sexual abuse. The flattering wolf-whistle becomes sexual harassment. The pile of dirty dishes in the sink no longer occasions self-rebuke and a sense of personal failure, but rather anger at an unreconstructed husband. It is not simply that the *interpretation* of the experience changes: the very experience and the emotions associated with it are different too. The apparent polarity between 'experience' and 'theory' is false: experience relies upon (explicit or implicit) theory, is always already theorised.

So when, in the Women's Studies classroom, someone (whether lesbian or heterosexual) complains that her 'experience' is being invalidated by the theories of sexuality under discussion, we cannot afford to allow that statement alone to stand in the way of developing those theories. Her comment should mark the *beginning* of a discussion, not the end of one. What is the implicit theory upon which her own (and other women's) experience is predicated? What personal investments does everyone have in particular theories? What would be the 'cost' of accepting some theories, rejecting others? In confronting feminist theories (whether offered by lesbian or by heterosexual feminists), experience is reinterpreted and this may feel liberating, illuminating, terrifying or invalidating, according to the nature and extent of one's prior theoretical commitments. The key issue here is not the authenticity of 'experience' judged against theory, but rather the political usefulness and implications of the theory *per se*.

The reclaiming of women's experience has been an important development for feminism, and for Women's Studies, and one which it is particularly important to hold fast to and to develop in the face of the obfuscatory abstractions of postmodernism. The developments needed require us to abandon the dogma of experiential authority, to be willing to challenge experience in ourselves and in others, to be willing to speak (and to hear others speak) without and beyond experience, and to imagine how our experience might be other than it currently is under heteropatriarchy. We cannot afford to be limited by experiential authority in creating a feminist transformation of the world.

References

Belenky, Mary, Blythe Clinchy, Nancy Goldberger and Jill Tarule (1986), *Women's Ways of Knowing: The Development of Self, Voice, and Mind* (New York: Basic Books).
Bhavnani, Kum Kum (1992), 'Talking Racism and the Editing of Women's Studies', in Diane Richardson and Vicki Robinson, eds, *Introducing Women's Studies* (London: Macmillan), pp. 27–48.
Bowles, Gloria and R. Duelli Klein, eds (1983) *Theories of Women's Studies* (London: Routledge & Kegan Paul).
Bunch, Charlotte (1975), 'Not for Lesbians Only', in *Quest: A Feminist Quarterly*, vol. 2, no. 2, pp. 78–94.
Coyner, Sandra (1983), 'Women's Studies as an Academic Discipline: Why and How to Do it', in Gloria Bowles and R. Duelli Klein, eds, *Theories of Women's Studies* (London: Routledge & Kegan Paul), pp. 46–71.
France, Marie (1983), 'Why Women's Studies?', in *Women's Studies International Forum*, vol. 6, no. 3, pp. 305–8.
Humm, Maggie (1991), '"Thinking of Things in Themselves": Theory, Experience, Women's Studies', in Jane Aaron and Sylvia Walby, eds, *Out of the Margins: Women's Studies in the Nineties* (London: Falmer), pp. 40–62.
Leeds Revolutionary Feminist Group (1981), 'Political Lesbianism: The Case Against Heterosexuality', in Onlywomen Press ed., *Love Your Enemy?: The Debate between Heterosexual Feminism and Political Lesbianism* (London: Onlywomen), pp. 1–8.
Livia, Anna (1989), 'You Can Only Be Wrong ...', in *Women's Review of Books*, vol. VI, nos. 10/11, pp. 33–4.
Nkweto Felly Simmonds, (1992), 'Difference, Power and Knowledge', in Hilary Hinds, Ann Phoenix and Jackie Stacey, eds, *Working Out: New Directions for Women's Studies* (London: Falmer), pp. 51–60.
Rich, Adrienne (1975), *On Lies, Secrets and Silence* (London: Virago).
—— (1980), 'Compulsory Heterosexuality and Lesbian Existence', in *Signs: Journal of Women in Culture and Society*, vol. 5, no. 4, pp. 631–60.
Wilkinson, Sue and Celia Kitzinger, eds (1993), *Heterosexuality: A 'Feminism & Psychology' Reader* (London: Sage).

12

Tropisms,[1] Tape-slide and Theory

MAGGIE HUMM

Theories about the personal – how identity is constructed and represented – are the stuff of Women's Studies. Questions about the work of sexual difference in our conscious and unconscious understandings of identity, and the relation between difference, identity and social and economic inequalities, are the specific questions which invite Women's Studies into the political arena. The processes by which individual women recognise themselves as female are often caught up in the compulsions of the visual. Indeed, the social face of femininity is constructed by mechanisms of visual representation, such as advertising and film, which gain women's collaboration and consent via specific forms of identification.

The personal signatures of women students/Women's Studies/media signs are thus in intimate political embrace. The power of politics resides in the production and dissemination of ideology, which in turn can rest on an ability to *re*-present the personal within a specific visual realm. The power of feminism resides in its ability to show how individual women are collectively constructed politically and usually oppressed. Feminist theory has made an incisive analysis of cinema and still images in terms of how viewing pleasures and subjectivity are gendered (for example, Mulvey 1975). Women's Studies in turn frequently addresses the power of media representations to explain the exact mechanisms which link political repression with subjectivity. Film/feminism/femininity are often the scene of Women's Studies as they are the scenic politics of society.[2]

The question which this chapter attempts to address, therefore, is how Women's Studies might purchase the political *through* new visual representations of the personal. More specifically, the chapter describes the utility of visual media for students' collective representations of the personal and their politics at the University of East London (UEL). The point is to situate the personal within a problematics of difference which student media work throws up.

145

Media Study at UEL

Since 1989 Women's Studies at UEL has collaborated with local community photographers in tape-slide courses.[3] Tape-slide is a cheap but potentially very powerful medium. Two or more carousel slide projectors, pulsed by a Gemini machine from a four- to eight-track audiotape, overlay still photographic images following a sequence of both spoken and musical sound. The sense of narrative combined with overlays or jarring juxtapositions is enhanced by music, poetry and personal stories.

The aim of this work is to teach media skills, utilising a high component of political, issue-based material. Women's Studies thus responds to both women's political concerns and to their future employment success as 'owners' of multitechnical skills (shooting, copying, editing, storyboard and soundtrack mixing). Collaborative work routines play a fundamental part, as do anti-racist working practices and disability awareness. Selecting images from magazines, newspapers and elsewhere and setting up joint photographic shoots in groups provides students with the opportunity to work collaboratively by pooling ideas and skills.

Media study is crucial to feminist cultural politics and hence to Women's Studies. First, the media are a major influence in women's perceptions of themselves and constructions of identity. All media create visual fantasies of and for particular subjectivities; for example, the Cadbury's chocolate Flake advertisements. Second, although there is currently a large body of feminist visual theory, from Laura Mulvey's pathbreaking essay 'Visual Pleasure and Narrative Cinema' onwards, *practices* of transformation have been little theorised and are often difficult to imagine. Feminist analysis of the power of media has been the task of a particular kind of theory – psychoanalysis. This has not, as yet, interrogated the *practices* of image construction as much as it interrogates the *reception* of those constructs. Tape-slide has a special purchase on both the political and the personal, because when we watch tape-slide we can see the *processes* of manufacture in the narrative sequences students choose to represent gendered, raced and classed identities. Both collective labour and an affirmation of a social/political message are figured in the process.

The title of the unit 'Women and the Visual Media' was consciously chosen over titles such as 'Women and Representation' or 'Images of Women'. The title immediately juxtaposes 'women' as signifier with the processes/institutions (visual media) which construct and attach representations to women, rather than, as in 'Images of Women' courses, panning superficially over a landscape of images. The unit, like all Women's Studies units, assumes that in order to subvert dominant representations it is crucial to understand how these work.

Perhaps not surprisingly, students choose to deploy the personal as their main subject material. Tapes creatively examine icons of mothering, reproductive technology and issues of weight and beauty, among others. Yet crucially, each time students locate personal representations in a political context, the latter does not absorb the former but sets up interesting tensions and dualisms.

In the production of student tape-slides the notion that 'the personal is political' is an intrinsic part of the medium. Students often enjoy reproducing personal material with a raw, rough, 'visible' editing style, delighting in the anti-élite, cheap, community conditions in which they work. They control the means of production. Unlike film, tape-slide inherently carries a hostility to commercial representations, by, for example, often disrupting cause-and-effect narratives and privileging everyday experience. Tape-slide *makes* the viewer think about the sequencing of events and the viewer's place in similar events. The disparity between sound and image highlights the message that the personal is not being smoothly *re*-presented *to* us, but is part of a process we create. Thus sound can dominate more than vision. Revealing disjunctions in address, tape-slide's anti-seamless process can be a visual politics.

Theory

In constructing a triad – film/feminism/femininity – we can witness a deployment of the problematics of the personal and the political which frequently plays itself out inside feminist thinking elsewhere. Two feminist theorists, Jacqueline Rose and Avtar Brah, have confronted these issues from different directions. Together both critics offer helpful ways of understanding the likely tensions between representations, politics and the personal.

Jacqueline Rose's *Sexuality in the Field of Vision* makes a feminist examination of the interface between the personal, sexual fantasy, the visual and psychoanalysis (Rose 1986). In her work Rose draws attention to the visual processes by which we learn and come to understand the meanings of sexual difference. Rose's critique of visual forms involves a questioning of sexual differences and the ways in which norms of representation 'reassuringly' stabilise these differences. Her argument, following Lacan, is that a fixed feminine identity is never possible in patriarchy.

Avtar Brah is a Ugandan Asian critic who has written extensively about the relation between race (as a visual signifier) and gender. In 'Questions of Difference and International Feminism' she argues that questions about cultural politics (in which we could include both the media and Women's Studies) should involve a 'politics of identification' rather than a 'politics of identity'. That is, Brah argues that the personal is always located within heterogeneous discursive processes. It is never a *given* intact identity.

For both critics, however, despite the very different disciplinary, ethnic and political positions they occupy, the scene of the personal is one in which processes of representation are fundamentally at issue. Artistic products (or tape-slide), argues Brah, should not be read as static symbols of cultural essentialism but as expressions of the *processes* of psychological and personal diversity. Rose agrees that we should pay careful attention to the *processes* of film as much as to the film product in order to challenge concepts of psychic identity with a political purpose.

In Women's Studies it is clear that the question of the personal brings with it fantasies and images of sexual difference. Students, like anyone else, recognise themselves in the fantasy formats of film and literature. Above all, students in Women's Studies are drawn to another question: how are representations of the personal (their mothers, children, bodies) tied to fantasies proffered by the media in order to limit women's political unconscious as well as our political actions? The issue of the representational *process* of the personal therefore leads outside the limits of curricular content to an understanding of how sexual difference is politically in play. The dialogue between media representations and feminism is a space where the larger political complexity of the personal is 'visible'.

Rose's *Sexuality in the Field of Vision* contains a sophisticated thinking through of the tension between representations of the title's two terms, 'sexuality' and 'vision'. The book's overall aim is twofold: first, to assess the important relation of psychoanalysis and feminism in contemporary political debate; and second, to assess how images of sexual difference at the heart of cultural institutions are tied to effects of the unconscious (or, we could claim, more generally to personal subjectivity). The book points out that Freud first made an indissoluble link between images and sexual difference in his 1910 essay 'Leonardo da Vinci and a

Memory of His Childhood'. Freud often relates the visual to sexual difference, constructing, for example, scenarios where moments of perception founder as boys refuse to believe anatomical differences or when the pleasure of looking becomes the excess of scopophilia. For Freud, Rose argues, the relation of viewer and scene is one of fracture. The representation of sexual difference has therefore less to do with the *content* of the scene and more to do with the subjectivity, and the *processes* of perception, of the viewer.

What Rose perceptively teases out is that the relation between sexuality (personal practices) and the image (the visual) are caught up in artistic processes because, following Lacan, we understand that sexual identities and their representations are fantasies. The problem for Rose is that in psychoanalysis, unlike in media work, the staging of sexual difference has *already taken place*. But *processes* of the visual are crucial because they can demonstrate oscillations in the domain of difference. Where Freud takes painting to be the *image* of the unconscious, post-Freudian thinking takes a more complex view. Representation is understood to be more abitrary. To postmodernists such as Meaghan Morris, representation is always a problem, never a reality.

The strength of Rose's work and its pertinence for Women's Studies is that she points to the dangers this cultural move entails. First, psychoanalytic concepts of the unconscious (the personal) are lost. Second, cultural artefacts are robbed of their values (politics). And third, the concept of textuality (or process) is taken away from sexual difference. Rose subtly suggests that *how* we see – the personal engagement with the image – belongs to 'a political intention'. Moreover, the 'intention is historical'. I am particularly intrigued by Rose's interest in process and 'mutual relation', because this relates to a debate about the issue of difference currently occupying feminist philosophers, sociologists and gender specialists.[4]

Avtar Brah's 'Questions of Difference and International Feminism' is a good example of these concerns. Brah's extensive research into British labour markets, Asian women and identity formation is too complex to summarise here. But in brief, she argues that respect for cultural difference (politics) is more likely if cultures are conceived less in terms of reified artefacts and more as processes. An important issue in Women's Studies is recognising the *processes* of women's diversity with regard to class, race and sexuality. The degree to which we can work across our differences may depend on conceptual representations drawing on the visual with which we understand those differences. As suggested above, rather than a politics of the personal – an identity politics – Brah persuasively suggests, we will better achieve coalitions through a politics of identification. That is, we often learn to see ourselves as part of imagined communities and we can identify with the politics of these groups without ever having been part of a specific history. Brah concludes that if cultural forms are conceived collectively, then cultural products are much less likely to be reified or essentialist. Cultural diversity, particularly in the media, encompasses an immense range of psychological and emotional expressions by reminding us, for example, that our personal experiences are not constituted solely within oppressions.

While Brah's focus is largely on the social, her suggestive concepts of 'imagined communities' and a 'politics of identification' are highly relevant to Rose's media concerns. Placing both accounts side by side we could argue that students' collective media practice within a feminist 'vision' might very well set up a 'mutual relation' between the unconscious and the social, between the personal and the political. The aim is to pull media work in the direction of recognising the political construction of the personal and back again to personal fantasies. The issue is to reconcile the personal with forms of representation which *in their process* recognise women's need for political change. Media study necessarily throws into question any division between an assumed 'real' world of politics and a fantasy/imagined existence of the personal, because it helps us think through how the political is always imagined 'phantastically'.

Problems with the 'Personal' in Early Women's Studies

In feminist circles during the 1970s the personal was defined largely in terms of personal oppressions and experiences of victimisation. In many teaching agendas in that decade a principal criterion of value was to enable learning to contribute to self-development. Experiential learning followed a model which began with the personal, then proceeded to reflection, analysis and evaluation of the personal. The purpose of Women's Studies in Britain then, as today, was empowerment. But 'empowerment' was often taken to mean simply the provision of a safe place for women – a space where women students and staff could share different experiences and personal realities in a safe environment (Kramarae and

Spender, 1992).[5] One example is the use of personal experience when reading literature, in order 'to be in touch with your feelings' (Hoffman 1985, p. 153). When describing personal experience students can make connections between private and public personas, can question the authenticity of public selves, can generate ideas about the nature of knowledge and authority.[6] An oscillation between the poles of the personal and political and the exploration of tensions between these poles can sometimes harness the personal as a means to educational reform, but it often becomes buried in the therapeutic so that means become ends.

Women's Studies is not unique in this regard. Personal growth movements characterised the educational worlds of the 1970s in a post-1960s belief that the steady extension of shared personal experiences would magically create an ideal education and a resulting transformation of society. Movements for educational reform such as humanistic psychology argue that the acquisition of positivistic scientific knowledge inhibits the personal changes needed to bring about social change (Halmos 1978, Rowan 1976, Robbins 1988). But, as Chandra Mohanty suggests, because issues of gender are contested differentially in different historical conjunctures, our theoretical constructs must come from 'the context being analysed', not simply from personal analysis (Mohanty 1984, p. 345). In other words, the empowerment of women is indissolubly linked to *discursive* contexts, which include the visual.

Tape-slide

The feminist subject of Women's Studies must therefore be less individual, less 'personal' and more a collective subject representing multiple and heterogeneous differences. Media work, by involving the multiple variables of viewer, subject and collective makers, sometimes simultaneously represents both dominant (white, able-bodied, etc) and dominated experience (sexual orientation, age and so forth). It is this sense of continuous and creative counterpoint between identifications (personal) and process (collective) which underpins media work. Engaged with the practical issues of costing and skills deployment, such study can never be accused of neglecting power forces because inevitably a media product is a historically specific result of particular production relations. Tape-slide addresses its own conditions of production and reception within the context of the personal.

A principal thread in contemporary feminism is its resistance to dominant representations of women in advertising, photography and film. Tape-slide images often start from the dominant but can establish unexpected juxtapositions between the bounded areas of high and popular culture; most obviously, for instance, by mixing family photos with slides of oil paintings. These defamiliarise the familiar as well as the family. It is the process of meaning-making which is crucial. Tape-slide offers a mediating 'neutrality' between life-world and social-world as the 'I' moves to 'we' and collective dialogue produces the possibility of new subjectivities.

One good example at UEL was *Beauty from Within*, a tape-slide dealing with issues of weight. Large and slim students photographed themselves and deconstructed dominant images from magazines, restaging moments of food obsession and the powerful forbiddens of femininity by deliberately emphasising the grotesqueries of size. The students speculated visually on how to be heavy women in a society which makes powerful heavy women unrepresentable. The tape-slide made a double move – of collective critique and playful/painful reconstruction – aiming to 'decensorise' the normative power of social representations. Thus statistical body measurements were overlaid on fantasy images combined with a strong voice-over reading a diary of bulimia. This combination impressively replaced the power of advertising. The tape-slide took up the critical challenges of both Rose and Brah: to *re*-present the *process* of 'mutual relation' between the personal and representations, and to create a 'politics of identification' with heavy women which any viewer could share. Self imagery was *not* the starting point but rather the collective work of identity creation.

Tape-slide can never be 'arty', because its multi-media 'crudity' inevitably challenges the concept of an immaculate art work. The personal as political often emerges more strongly through tape-slide than it does through other photographic genres. Removed from its traditional school base and placed instead within a feminist agenda, tape-slide is sometimes eccentric in its technical execution if precise in its intention, but its preoccupation with juxtaposition allows its role as a *political* process to be registered. The aberrant use of advertisements and readings against the grain are often compelling. The construction of *de*construction sets loose a range of unintended associations, by their nature invalidating transparent reality. There is no 'painterly' gesture.

Tape-slide offers a great flexibility and potential for dislocating existing regimes of political representations and for constructing new multiplicities of knowledges. If one of the stylistic norms of magazines and advertising, for example, is a constant deployment of a fleeting, *arrested* 'woman' and a liberal reduction of femininity to the phenomenal, then tape-slide offers continuous flowing of superimpositions and multiplicity. Tape-slide's 'photomontage' distorts the physical while at the same time displaying recognisable people and objects, and inviting political thinking through visual effects. The juxtapositions of original photographs and advertisements create fractured images of femininity and graphically portray the motley and multiple ways in which women experience the personal.

Tropisms

Other tape-slides addressed the question of the visual in itself, for instance high art's representation of mothering. *Reproducing Ourselves* aimed to display figurative, representational art from the Renaissance to the present in order to show how the personal experience of mothering is never satisfactorily represented (Rich 1977). Yet the work deconstructed itself by revealing an interplay between students' unconscious desire *for* motherhood with the conscious political activity of investigating 'motherhood'. The powerful visual juxtapositions of Bellini's paintings with *Prima* stereotypes contrasted oddly with strangely mood-enhancing music of strong triads. It was no surprise to learn several months later that one of these graduating students, an Italian, had given birth.

Tape-slides often bring up unspoken and repressed experiences (tropisms), here for example a desire to mother, making visual knowledge about topics that are central to feminist politics.

Studying Women: Five Student Autobiographies gained political strength from representing both the attractions of domesticity and its dreariness. What clearly made the tape-slide political was its politicisation of domestic issues, including sexual abuse. On the one level the chosen images were personal – domestic objects – appropriate to a very personal event. On the other hand, the tape-slide made the 'personal' 'political' by accompanying these images with a strong plea for more public means of telling. The tape-slide was organised around the need to tell. Words printed on gels were superimposed on images at regular points. The message varied in graphic style, size and duration and broke with a narrative continuity. The graphic information carried its own resonances and associations, matching and mismatching the gentle voice-over. The direct personal moments placed the viewer in contact with a *positional* politics. Words and images clarified, or sometimes undercut, each other and, enhanced by the compulsions of soundtrack and darkened viewing space, the personal gained a public credibility. The re-presentation of the personal allowed new political questions to emerge about family histories, sexual practices and identity.

As a result of her identification of the issues involved in cinematic determinisms, Rose articulates what a feminist politics of representation must address: the collision between a feminism drawn to images from the personal with a technological apparatus involving an optics of realism and perfect reproducability gaining the consent of the unconscious. 'Putting the concept of sexual difference back into discussion of the cinematic apparatus', she argues, is the problem of cinema, but the question of process which this inevitably entails could be part of the solution (Rose 1986, p. 213).

Tape-slide undercuts the idea of untramelled unconscious determinations. It might perhaps be fruitful to realign and to establish tape-slide as a film form operating within socially and historically produced visual processes, since the principle of juxtaposition at the heart of tape-slide is similar to the principle of montage in the cinema. But in tape-slide certain kinds of juxtaposition are uniquely possible. For Women's Studies, the possibility of working with the interpellation of the unconscious (through processes of camera projection) and *subverting* these processes by contrasting the visual with a distanced scripto-audio offers the possibility of political art. As the viewer moves from subject position to subject position, 'historical specificity and universalism need not be counterposed against each other' (Brah 1991, p. l74). As students work collectively, swapping skills and blurring authorship, the film form and political content work together, changing ideas of political art.

Conclusion

What I have been trying to convey with these examples from one Women's Studies course is the way in which visual processes can be exploited to create representations which operate on several levels, from the personal to political thought and visual pleasure. The core of Women's Studies work is a struggle with representations and with established forms of knowledge which align the personal with representative (or unrepresentative) social identities. To deconstruct and disavow the domain of false self-recognitions involves applying a constant pressure of something repressed: the personal – something that can come sharply into focus through alternative practices. In addition, Asian, Black and white students open up a visual space for images normally marginalised or made invisible in traditional curricula. They control both the *means* of production – slide projectors, tape-recorders, cameras – and the *forms* of representation – the images and languages of, for instance, anti-racism. With tape-slide, students undertake the political task of addressing social isssues in a public way while making visible and legitimate their personal views and lives.

The affinity between film/feminism/female cannot of course in itself create political change, but, equally, recognition of this affinity in the domain of collective practices could reveal the fallibility of traditional knowledges. All this is well-covered ground. What remains important is that a recontextualisation of personal experience and the move from the personal as private to the personal as publicly visible raises issues about the relation between the two. Of course, as Lucy Lippard realistically argues, the visual is no more than a 'functioning element in society' (Lippard 1980). But if the function of the *feminist* visual is to open up political possibilities, then who knows what new images of our persons and of our politics we may see?

Notes

1. 'Tropisms': 'In author Nathalie Sarraute's work, a term devised for her attempt to record experience as it is felt before it passes through the filter of language' (Kramarae and Treichler 1985, p. 459).
2. Pollock (1992) charts this trajectory in the realm of visual culture, arguing that analysis cannot use a single disciplinary frame of reference. Hence the utility of Women's Studies. See also Kelly 1977.
3. Since 1988 the Independent Photography Project (TIPP), Woolwich, has produced more than 50 tape-slides. From 1989 onwards, TIPP has tutored an audiovisual module in the Women's Studies degree at UEL. The breadth of TIPP's feminist vision and artistic skills are due entirely to the expertise of

its professional photographers and audiotechnicians: Trish le Gal, Santoshni Perara, Linda Conboy.

4. Feminist discussions of epistemological processes, particularly in science for example, draw attention to the ways in which experience and analysis are not dichotomous but interactive, in that all analysis is shaped by the political context and conjectures of the viewer (Bleier 1986, Collins 1990, Harding 1987, Hirsch and Fox Keller 1990, Pateman and Gross 1986, Smith 1987, Stanley 1990).

5. The concept of a 'woman-centered perspective' is frequently proposed but its precise *methodology* is still unfocused. Following Bowles and Duelli Klein (1983), feminist thinking has fractured into a poststructuralist rejection of the essentialism inherent in such a perspective (Riley, 1984); attacks on the ethnocentrism implied by its exclusions (Spelman 1988, Spivak 1987); psychoanalytic (Lacanian) attacks on a unified perspective (Mitchell and Rose 1982); and anxieties about the heterosexism of a singular perspective (Fuss 1991). Yet a desire to retain the category for feminist analysis is felt very strongly, not least by students entering Women's Studies. Attempts to define a feminist-standpoint epistemology have been more thoroughgoing in Sociology, particularly in Stanley's work (1990).

6. I have written elsewhere (Humm 1991) of the possible dangers involved in encouraging students to deny their social subjectivities by allowing the work of academic deconstruction to become their new 'identity'.

References

Bleier, Ruth, ed. (1986), *Feminist Approaches to Science* (New York: Pergamon).

Bowles, Gloria and Renate Duelli Klein, eds (1983), *Theories of Women's Studies* (London: Routledge).

Brah, Avtar (l991), 'Questions of Difference and International Feminism', in Jane Aaron and Sylvia Walby, eds, *Out of the Margins: Women's Studies in the Nineties* (London: Falmer).

Collins, Patricia (1990), *Black Feminist Thought* (London: Unwin Hyman).

Fuss, Diana, ed. (1991) *Inside/Out: Lesbian Theories, Gay Theories* (London: Routledge).

Halmos, Paul (1978), *The Faith of the Counsellors*, (London: Constable).

Harding, Sandra, ed. (1987), *Feminism and Methodology* (Milton Keynes: Open University Press).

Hirsch, Marianne and Evelyn Fox Keller, eds (1990), *Conflicts in Feminism* (London: Routledge).

Hoffman, Nancy Jo (1985), 'Breaking Silences: Life in the Feminist Classroom', in Margo Culley and Catherine Portuges, eds, *Gendered Subjects: The Dynamics of Feminist Teaching* (London: Routledge).

Humm, Maggie (1991), '"Thinking of Things in Themselves": Theory, Experience, Women's Studies', in Jane Aaron and Sylvia Walby, eds, *Out of the Margins: Women's Studies in the Nineties* (London: Falmer).

Kelly, Mary (1977), 'On Sexual Politics and Art', reprinted in Rozsika Parker and Griselda Pollock, eds, *Framing Feminism: Art and the Women's Movement 1970–85* (London: Pandora, 1987).

Kramarae, Cheris and Paula Treichler (1985), *A Feminist Dictionary* (London: Pandora).

Kramarae, Cheris and Dale Spender (1992), *The Knowledge Explosion: Generations of Feminist Scholarship* (New York: Teachers College Press).

Lippard, Lucy (1980), 'Issue and Tabu', in *Issue: Social Strategies by Women Artists* (London: ICA).

Mitchell, Juliet and Jacqueline Rose (1982), *Feminine Sexuality: Jacques Lacan and the Ecole Freudienne* (London: Macmillan).

Mohanty, Chandra (1984), 'Under Western Eyes: Feminist Scholarship and Colonial Discourses', in *Boundary*, vol. 2, nos. 12–13 (3), pp. 333–58.

Mulvey, Laura (1975), 'Visual Pleasure and Narrative Cinema', in *Screen*, vol. 16, p. 3.

Pateman, Carole and Elizabeth Gross, eds (1986), *Feminist Challenges: Social and Political Theory* (Sydney: Allen & Unwin).

Pollock, Griselda (1992), 'Trouble in the Archives: Introduction', in *Differences*, vol. 4, no. 3, pp. iii–xiv.

Rich, Adrienne (1977), *Of Woman Born* (London: Virago).

Riley, Denise (1984), *Am I That Name? Feminism and the Category of 'Woman' in History* (London: Macmillan).

Robbins, Derek (1988), *The Rise of Independent Study* (Milton Keynes: SRHE and Open University Press).

Rose, Jacqueline (1986), *Sexuality in the Field of Vision* (London: Verso).

Rowan, John (1976), *Ordinary Ecstasy: Humanistic Psychology in Action* (London: Routledge, Kegan & Paul).
Smith, Dorothy (1987), *The Everyday World as Problematic: A Feminist Sociology* (Boston, MA: North Eastern University Press).
Spelman, Elizabeth, V. (1988), *Inessential Women: Patterns of Exclusion in Feminist Thought* (Boston, MA: Beacon).
Spivak, Gayatri (1987), *In Other Worlds: Essays in Cultural Politics* (London: Methuen).
Stanley, Liz, ed. (1990), *Feminist Praxis: Research,Theory and Epistemology in Feminist Sociology* (London: Routledge).

13
Reading as Autobiography

LYNNE PEARCE

In 1992 I presented a paper at the 'Feminist Methodologies' Conference in London entitled '"I the Reader": Text, Context, and the Balance of Power'.[1] The paper was well received at the time, but I had no idea that it was to prove so useful in pedagogical terms. For this autobiographical 'reader's history' – a testament to my own 'changing experience' as student, teacher and literary critic – had the effect of prompting all those groups with whom I have shared it into reviewing their own experiences as 'gendered readers'. It produced a collective desire to remember when it was that they first became aware that certain texts were excluding them, others embracing them, and when they began to affirm/resist this 'positioning' with a feminist conciousness.

As the result of witnessing the popularity of the 'reader's autobiography' in a number of very different academic contexts (ranging from undergraduate seminars on women's writing and literary theory, to MA and other graduate fora, to a staff research group), I have come to realise that it might function as a useful group exercise: a means of enabling women readers at all stages of their lives and academic careers to examine their reading practice from a newly self-reflexive methodological perspective. As a methodology, indeed, the construction of 'reader-autobiographies' has the advantage of enabling participants to confront, through the 'authority' of their own experience, big theoretical issues; such as whether the gender of an author *necessarily* affects the gender-positioning of his or her text. This is not to say that the experience of any one individual can then be presented as *bona fide* 'evidence' on the subject, but the self-inclusive mechanism at least enables everyone (including students generally lacking in confidence when confronted with theoretical issues) to engage in the debate. Clearly any claims to 'authority' based on such subjective, experiential data can only be countenanced if the individuals concerned then go on to compare their 'testimonies' within larger groups, but the process of theorisation will have begun from a standpoint to which everyone has contributed.

Before pursuing the theoretical and pedagogical possibilities of reader-autobiographies any further, however, I want first to present my own. What follows is an attempt to summarise in about 1,500 words information that in my original paper took 5,000; but I see this as an exercise that will, I hope, provide readers of this chapter with a model on which to base their own autobiographies, even allowing for the fact that some will feel they have less of a 'history' to tell than others.

The Story so Far

Like most of us, I was first 'trained' in the art of reading while at school, and my courses in 'O' and 'A' level English Literature presented the author (almost invariably male) as the (reverential) source of a text's 'meaning'. As adolescent and often adulating female readers of these texts, we were taught to engage 'sensitively' with the humanist principles of whichever author was under consideration and (most importantly) to suspend all recognition of our own gendered identities. As I explain elsewhere (Pearce 1994a), the common practice of those of us faced with the work of James Joyce, D.H. Lawrence or William Shakespeare was to compensate for the fact that these were texts blatantly exclusive of a female audience by becoming 'transvestite readers': learning to respond, whatever the text/context, as universalised male subjects and 'identifying' with the most improbable male characters.

If, however, the first phase of my reader's history can be excused on the grounds of youthful ignorance and Leavisite[2] brainwashing, the same cannot apply to the muddle I continued to make of things once my feminist consciousness had been 'raised'. While my undergraduate years at university saw me engaged in a basic continuation of the humanist enterprise, despite a few interesting (but politically unaccountable) scrapes with literary theory, my postgraduate years saw me change from a 'transvestite' reader into a schizoidly 'bisexual' one. The reason for this is that my emerging interest in women's writing and feminist theory was virtually co-terminous with the start of my PhD on the later poems of the early nineteenth-century peasant poet John Clare (Pearce 1987), and the next five years saw me jumping from one readerly/scholarly persona to another without any real recognition of the political dubiousness of my enterprise. Although I was teaching overtly feminist courses by this time, the 'deconstruction' of images of women in nineteenth-century art and literature failed to impinge upon my reading of Clare. This can be explained partly because my initial interest in Clare's manuscripts was largely formal and stylistic. Inspired by the work of the Russian critic Mikhail Bakhtin (Bakhtin 1984), I focused on the 'polyphony' ('multivoicedness') of Clare's texts and failed to observe the gendered power-play between speakers and addressees *within* the text, or even how the text was excluding me as a female reader.[3] Indeed, the contemporary critical vogue for 'reader-power' (the author is 'dead'/the meaning of the text is the property of the reader) made me feel supremely in control of my material (Pearce 1994a).[4] I believed that it was my readerly 'actualisation' that was enabling surprising things about Clare's poems to be made visible for the first time.[5] This might indeed have been the case; but it completely ignored the gendered power the text had *over me* as a female reader.

Yet this 'gender-blind' work with Clare and Bakhtin was, as I have already indicated, bizarrely juxtaposed with my simultaneous teaching and writing on the Pre-Raphaelites. The book *Woman/Image/Text* (Pearce 1991a) which eventually came out of this engagement began life as a violent reaction against texts (this time, paintings) which I experienced as excluding and demeaning to me as a female viewer. Although the thesis on which the finished book depends takes a more subtle line by arguing that *despite* their overt sexual/textual positioning these are images that can be read 'against the grain', it is important to register that the project was motivated by some very unsophisticated emotions. For the first time, the extent to which certain texts (visual or verbal) can exclude/patronise/denigrate their female audiences had really hit home with me. And yet (to bring this particular phase of my reader's history to a close) Clare escaped my chagrin without so much as a flip across the ear.

Although the theoretical, ethical and political questions raised by the Pre-Raphaelite book (in particular, to what extent is it legitimate for the twentieth-century feminist to 'appropriate' male-produced texts outside the context of their original production/consumption?) took some time to work through, it is necessary that I now move on to the third and most recent chapter of my 'reader's history', which concerns my involvement with women's writing.

To cut the long intervening story short, the end of all my theoretical agonising was to leave the problems of nineteenth-century male-authored texts behind me and turn, with relief, to the study of contemporary feminist literature. Here (I argued to myself and to my students) were texts that, whatever their own aesthetic and political problems, were at least *addressed* to me: texts which directed themselves to an audience that was not only 'female' but 'feminist'. Indeed, I quickly established this cognition as the basis for a new definition of what we might mean by 'women's writing': women's writing (at least, that which would call itself 'feminist') is best understood not as writing by women, nor as writing about them, but as writing *for* them (Pearce 1992). This was a period of great readerly liberation for me (Pearce 1994a). After years of struggling to make positive readings of 'resistant' texts, it was a wonderful relief to turn to works that not only included but *privileged* the woman reader. Indeed, if I were to follow my earlier analogy through, it is clear that this was the moment when I changed from being a 'bisexual' reader into a self-consciously 'lesbian' one; not in the sense that I was interested in reading only lesbian or lesbian-authored texts, but (to adapt Adrienne Rich's definition of lesbianism – Rich 1986) because my primary 'emotional' commitment was now to texts which specified and privileged relationships with women readers.

The immediate euphoria produced by this discovery of texts that appeared to be addressed specifically to me was, however, short-lived. Even though I thought at first that by defining 'women's writing' in terms of 'readership' rather than 'authorship' I avoided the problematic essentialism associated with the latter, I soon discovered that even a 'dialogic' relationship[6] between text and reader still essentialised women (that is, the female audience) as a group. It was clearly naive and utopian to believe that *all* women could be included in/represented by the address of any one text, even if that address were gender-specific. Differences of age, class, race, nationality and sexuality are as present in groups of women readers as they are in the population at large. This theoretical realisation was augmented by my own (painful) feelings of 'rejection' by certain feminist texts: an emotional recognition that I have described as 'reader-jealousy'. As I observe in '"I the Reader"': 'The text I had thought of as "mine" was talking to others as easily as it talked to me' (Pearce 1994a).

Although I would still situate myself in this third phase of my reader's autobiography, I have fortunately found a means of rationalising this 'reader-jealousy'. This rationalisation depends upon the realisation that although texts may have multiple addressees (such as a range of class, race and sexuality positionings), this does not mean that they will operate without preference or discrimination. As Stuart Hall discovered in his work with television discourse more than 20 years ago (Hall 1980), all textual communication operates a code of hierarchy vis-à-vis its audiences; meaning that some readers will, in any one text, be more privileged than others. Far from being depressed by evidence of this discrimination I found that, with respect to my own experience as a reader, it helped both to explain the *source* of my emotions (jealousy/betrayal) and to promise that while I would, indeed, be marginalised or excluded by some reader-positionings, I would be privileged and embraced by others.

To conclude, it was the realisation that the 'reader-experience' is a volatile and unpredictable roller-coaster that has made me *more* prepared to accept the risks involved every time I open a new book. Whether authored by a man or a woman, whether purportedly 'feminist' or not, there is no assurance either way of how someone of my particular gender, age, race, class or sexuality will be positioned; or, indeed, what room there will be for collusion with/resistance to this positioning. And so my reader's history finds me, in the present, both more vulnerable and more 'prepared' than ever before. I have learnt to accept the possibility of rejection alongside that of co-option, and to recognise that both are part of the total 'reader-experience'.

The Reader's Experience

In reviewing the above summary of my reader's history, I was especially struck by the new way in which 'experience' is configured within the text–reader relationship. In earlier feminist literary criticism, the reader's experience was discussed (and subsequently discounted) largely in the context of 'authentic realism': the type of reading practice now associated with the consciousness-raising groups of the 1970s where literature would be used as a way of exploring and challenging the 'common experiences' of women's lives (for instance menstruation, marriage, childbirth, menopause), and would consequently be 'evaluated' according to its 'authenticity' relative to 'real life' (Mills 1989). The notion of 'reader-experience' that emerges from my own autobiography is quite different in that the experience is located not in the reader's *life*, but in her ('dialogic') engagement with the text. For the feminist literary critic, concern thus moves away from the 'authentic' *representation* of experience within the text, to the reader's experience of the text. How does a particular text gender and otherwise 'identify' its audience? How 'included' and 'comfortable' does it make us feel? Does its positioning make us want to 'give up' or 'read on'? To what extent does it allow us to challenge or resist its positioning? This, I would suggest, is ultimately a far more productive way of approaching the question of experience vis-à-vis readership than getting newly embroiled in the issue of whether literature can or should 'reflect' the conditions of our material existence.

Uses of the Autobiography

I would like to conclude by briefly suggesting some ways in which students and teachers might make use of the 'reader's autobiography' in research or teaching seminar groups.

First, as I noted earlier, there are evident advantages in such an exercise being undertaken as part of a group, since, by comparing experiences, participants will probably feel able to engage with the issues at a theoretical level with greater confidence. While no individual is likely, for example, to problematise Wolfgang Iser's theory of the 'implied reader' (Iser 1978) through her or his own isolated example, a consensus opinion among the group might lead to a serious (and well-substantiated) challenge.

It is the kind of exercise, too, that works well to bring groups together. In my own experience, this was most noticeable in the feminist research group to which I belong. The presentation of my own 'reader's history' in confidential, autobiographical terms seemed to enable other members of the group to discuss their own theoretical premises and methodologies more frankly than before. This may be partly because most of us find it less intimidating to explain the *processes* through which we have arrived at our present critical/theoretical/methodological position than simply to justify it. Whatever the reason, it seems to be an exercise that few group members can ultimately resist participating in: once you've told someone your reader's history, they will want to tell you theirs.

Following on from this last point, I would also suggest that any teacher thinking of using the exercise in a seminar should begin by sharing her own reader's history with the group (or, alternatively, using mine). This is because the prospect of any writing exercise is intimidating in the abstract, but quite accessible once the individuals concerned see how they might begin to 'write themselves in'. What makes the autobiographical mode more facilitating than most for such an exercise is the ease with which we are all able to narrativise our pasts, and this evidently applies to intellectual retrospectives as much as to personal ones. Even students at the beginning of their reader-histories will have at least the beginnings of a narrative. On the other hand, if more mature students find the prospect of writing a full reader's autobiography too demanding in the time available (were the exercise to take place in a half-hour seminar, for example), there is also the option of getting them to write about their changing response to a *particular text*: how they have read and reread *Wuthering Heights* (1847) or *Sons and Lovers* (1913) at different stages of their lives, for instance.

On the question of gender, it is important to emphasise to any group about to undertake the exercise that there is no expectation their own trajectory will necessarily follow mine or anyone else's. This is especially important to stress to groups that are already identified as 'feminist', since the participants might feel the pressure to construct a 'politically correct' profile for themselves (for example, 'stopped reading D.H. Lawrence in early twenties/now prefer Jeanette Winterson'). An instance of this type of anxiety presented itself to me recently when a member of one of my MA groups confessed to me, after a class in which we had been discussing these issues, that she still preferred reading male authors, partly *because* of the very marginalisation/alienation she experienced as a woman reader. She explained that it gave her a particular pleasure to enter a world in which no efforts had been made to 'accommodate' her. While this will undoubtedly seem a perverse position to many of you, there will certainly be others for whom it will strike a chord. Furthermore, in terms of a group exercise it is just the sort of dissent that should be welcomed if a serious debate over the implications of gendered reading is to take place.

It is important to recognise too that the reader's autobiography can be used to explore more than just the gendered positioning of text and reader. The focus of my own original autobiography (Pearce 1994a), which has been somewhat marginalised in the summary account reproduced here, was an examination of the relative power of author, text and reader in the production of meaning. This is an important issue for all students of literary theory and criticism to grasp as early on in their careers as possible, and the reader's autobiography is, I find, one of the best ways of enabling them to reflect upon the larger issues at stake in a non-threatening way. Barthes' 'death of the author' (Barthes 1977), for instance, often proves a difficult concept when presented as an abstract theory, but if readers have first been asked to reflect upon their own role in the production of a text's meaning it will seem rather less startling. In addition, the exercise can most profitably be used as a basis for exploring *to what extent* the reader supplies a text's meaning. Is she the omnipotent resident of one of Stanley Fish's 'interpretive communities' (Fish 1980),[7] for example, or simply, in Wolfgang Iser's terms, an 'actualiser'? (Iser 1978).

Assuming, however, that readers of this book – students and teachers alike – will be most interested in the possibilities of the reader-autobiography from a gendered perspective, may I end by suggesting that, as an exercise, one of its great merits is that it admits an emotional dimension to what is commonly perceived as a purely intellectual activity. The reader's autobiography, as my own has shown, offers each of us the possibility of exploring the conflicts and contradictions of our reader-positioning through the feelings of excitement, power, jealousy and relief that have accompanied the confusion. It is an exercise which permits us to re-examine, in the raw, what it has meant to us to be positioned as a female reader or viewer of a text; to be honest about what we felt then and what (in the light of newly acquired theoretical sophistications) we think we *ought* to feel now. Most of all, writing our own reader-histories helps us come to terms with the fact that even as texts effect multiple reader-positionings so have we responded with multiple reader-responses (Pearce 1994a). How we change and develop as feminist readers is a profile quite as complex as our lifelong negotiation of femininity, sexuality or any other of the social and political factors by which we are inscribed. And for me, as a feminist academic, it remains one of the most fascinating areas of intellectual experience there is.

Notes

1   This conference was held at the Institute of Romance Studies, University of London, in January 1992 and was organised by Penny Florence and Dee Reynolds. A book based on the conference proceedings is edited by the organisers (Florence and Reynolds 1994).
2   'Leavisite': an allusion to the school of literary criticism associated with the work of F.R. Leavis which evaluated literature in terms of its humanist ideals and was trenchantly

opposed to modernity, the growth of mass culture, and all politically motivated criticisms such as Marxism.

3 I have subsequently attempted to redress this omission in a feminist retrospective on my work with Clare (Pearce 1991b)

4 'Death of the Author': see Roland Barthes' essay of 1968, reproduced in his *Image-Music-Text* (Barthes 1977). In this celebrated essay Barthes rejects the traditional humanist view of the author as the source of the text's meaning and proposes that readers are free to 'enter the text from any direction' (Selden 1985, p. 75).

5 'Actualisation': see Wolfgang Iser (1978). According to Iser, the literary text is comprised of a network of semantic 'gaps' which the reader is required to 'actualise' into meaning.

6 'Dialogic': this concept derives from the work of Mikhail Bakhtin (1984), who believed that all utterances (written and spoken) were a 'two-sided act' dependent upon the presence of a speaker and a reciprocating addressee. As a model, dialogism has also been used to help explain the mutual interdependence of texts and readers in the creation of meaning. For further information see Holquist 1990 and Pearce 1994b.

7 'Interpretive community': in his famous essay *Is There a Text in this Class?*, Stanley Fish (1980) proposes that readers make sense of texts according to the norms and competencies of their own sociohistorical reading community.

References

Bakhtin, Mikhail (1984), *Problems of Dostoevsky's Poetics* (Manchester: Manchester University Press, 1984).

Barthes, Roland (1977), 'The Death of the Author' in *Image-Music-Text*, trans. Stephen Heath (London: Fontana), pp. 142–8.

Fish, Stanley (1980), *Is There a Text in this Class?* (Cambridge, MA: Harvard University Press).

Florence, Penny and Dee Reynolds (1994), *Media/Subject/Culture: Feminist Positions and Redefinitions* (Manchester: Manchester University Press).

Hall, Stuart (1980), 'Encoding/Decoding', in *Culture, Media, Language* (London: Hutchinson), pp. 128–38.

Holquist, Michael (1990), *Dialogism: Bakhtin and His World* (London: Methuen).

Iser, Wolfgang (1978), *The Act of Reading: A Theory of Aesthetic Response* (Baltimore: John Hopkins University Press).

Mills, Sara (1989), 'Authentic Realism', in S. Mills, L. Pearce, S. Spaull and E. Millard, eds, *Feminist Readings/Feminists Reading*, (Hemel Hempstead: Harvester Wheatsheaf), pp. 51–82.

—— ed. (1994), *Gendering the Reader* (Hemel Hempstead: Harvester Wheatsheaf).

Pearce, L. (1987), 'John Clare and Mikhail Bakhtin – The Dialogic Principle' unpublished PhD thesis, (Birmingham University).

—— (1991a), *Woman/Image/Text: Readings in Pre-Raphaelite Art and Literature* (Hemel Hempstead: Harvester Wheatsheaf).

—— (1991b) 'John Clare's *Child Harold*: The Road Not Taken', in Susan Sellers, ed., *Feminist Criticism: Theory and Practice*, (Hemel Hempstead: Harvester Wheatsheaf), pp. 143–56.

—— (1992), 'Dialogic Theory and Women's Writing', in Hilary Hinds, Ann Phoenix and Jackie Stacey, eds, *Working Out: New Directions for Women's Studies*, (London: Falmer), pp. 184–93.

—— (1994a) '"I the Reader": Text, Context, and the Balance of Power', in Penny Florence and Dee Reynolds, eds, *Media/Subject/Culture: Feminist Positions and Redefinitions* (Manchester: Manchester University Press).

—— (1994b), *Reading Dialogics* (London: Edward Arnold).

Rich, Adrienne (1986), 'Compulsory Heterosexuality and Lesbian Existence', in *Blood, Bread and Poetry* (London: Virago), pp. 23–75.

Selden, Raman (1985), *A Reader's Guide to Contemporary Literary Theory* (Brighton: Harvester).

14

Video Practice within the Academy[1]

PENELOPE KENRICK

Not only does the address of women's art speak one-to-one, but the content of the work often describes an individual experience of another human being – a mother, a son, a lover, even a specified oppressor. The political and the economic forces of our society are still experienced by women through their individual relationships, both inside and outside the home. The exploration of the personal, of one-to-one within a work of art, remains a potent expression of the feminist enterprise. (Elwes 1990, p. 31)

Catherine Elwes, a leading feminist video-maker since the 1970s, places the personal at the root of feminist creative endeavour, and for her the personal is most aptly expressed through the use of video. It brings together words (writing and speech), photography and performance in intimate cohesion. The complex relationships between expressions of the body, the pleasures of visual representations 'beyond words' and an articulated representation through words are manifest in this medium, allowing a rich exploration of meanings, both layered and open. The simultaneous representations of the bodily, the visual and the verbal through time could be seen as closer to personal experience than the use of the written text on the page. It is, perhaps, this inclusiveness and multiplicity that attracts some women to the use of video when exploring feminist issues for themselves, drawing on material from their own lives and those of women around them.

I want to start by looking at the unique qualities of video as a medium in relation to written text or film, and then to show that those qualities have advantages for feminist practice and use in Women's Studies, particularly when working within the conventions of the academic institution. I would like to include an outline of how video-production has been used by students on our course at Anglia Polytechnic University and to show, by citing examples, how they engage in a range of practices and illustrate different ways in which the personal is integrated with the social and the private with the public, which may encourage others to use this medium to express feminist concerns.

Video and Literature

It is inappropriate to discuss video as an equivalent to a series of still images; it is much closer to written text in the continuity of representations and the building up of a full narrative over a period of time. However, writers on Cultural Studies have been at pains to point out the differences between the written text and the moving image (whether it be film, TV or video), as they have felt that literary conventions have dominated the interpretations or readings of the moving image. Fiske and Hartley state:

> We live in a society where literacy and its associated skills and modes of thought are valued very highly. This means that the tendency to judge all media, including T.V., by the prescriptions of literacy is not the result of mere intellectual confusion. Rather it is a reflection of the dominant cultural values, instilled during 500 years of print-literacy. (Fiske and Hartley 1989, p. 15)

There was, and perhaps still is, a tendency to treat the moving image as literature with pictures, and to place it within existing conventions of literary criticism (Turner 1988, p. 37). This 'illustrative' function is a dominant mode of reading video in educational institutions today. Cubitt sets out a background to the debate on the differences between video and its reception, and the written text and its reader: 'The mysteries surrounding literary text still reek of the Book at the heart of Western Culture, the Bible: creation, inspiration, genius, being faithful to the text ... Silent reading is more like a prayer, head bowed in silent, lonely subjugation' (Cubitt 1991, p. 2). He raises the importance of the spoken word in relation to the viewer. Speech has a direct, physical projection and emotional force and the viewer has an active response to it. Cubitt wants to enhance the position of the viewer by stressing her active role, her ability to transform the text/image through interpretation, and to emphasise that 'reading' is not synonymous for book, play, film, fashion or video.

Video (and other moving images) can potentially subvert the values most prized by literary academicism. It can be a 'dangerous weapon' in that context. It can be inconsistent, ephemeral, episodic with no clear narrative; it may have no authoritative voice; it can be created from momentary juxtapositions of sound and vision. For example, one student made a short piece using video material that had been accumulated collectively and relatively sponta- neously by four students working together over a weekend. She selected from that material to create a poetic evocation around an individual. Phrases from a passing conversation were captured, layered, and repeated; they expressed in an eliptical way the tensions of living as a feminist. The images showed momentary sensuous views of fingers working red ochre over a woman's stomach juxtaposed with glimpses of intimate corners in a woman's house and close shots of gesturing hands, presenting a suggestive portrait which drew on strands that were personal and collective. Both simple and complex, this short piece was simultaneously direct and elusive, and difficult to evaluate in terms of literary convention. It is significant that the development of a theoretical discourse on the moving image occurred first in journals such as *Screen*, outside the academic institution. Discussion of the moving image soon became part of the wider, multidisciplinary field of Cultural Studies, involving linguistics, semiotics, psychoanalysis, anthro- pology, sociology, social history and feminism. A summary of debates about the relation of feminism to the reading of the moving image may be found in Kuhn (1982, pp. 3–18).

The written text has only one system of signification, with a convention of grammatical structure. The moving image, however, has no 'grammar', no system of order or sequence that must be followed. There is no simple parallel between a single shot and a written sentence. The relationship between images and sound is extremely fluid, complex and multiple. The signifying systems include camera angles, length of shot, lighting, colour/tone, sound, *mis-en-scène* (spatial relationships, details of setting and so on) and, importantly, editing. Each of these has a set of conventions that can be used, played with, undermined or replaced (Turner 1988, p. 49).

On the one hand, video production within the academy is still relatively novel and therefore the weight of historical convention that might discourage innovation has not yet gathered around its production and analysis. But on the other hand, it is too easily assumed that because of its difference from written academic texts, it cannot be taken seriously as an academic practice and cannot be easily assessed. However, video-readers and -makers are intensely 'literate' (Cubitt 1991, p. 3); we are members of a culture in which the moving image has taken a prominent role in our lives. In fact, we are so familiar with making judgements about the complex codes and conventions of visual material we encounter in everyday experience that we take it for granted. But we find it difficult to transfer that confidence to the academic context, perhaps because of the pervasive literary conventions.

Video and Film

Video is seen as the least respectable of the media (Cubitt 1991, p. 16). However, its marginalised position has advantages for feminist production. Using it, feminists can question the tyranny of professional expectations found in film and TV and they can critique representations of gender that dominate those media. The danger of course is that if video itself is marginalised, these critiques too may remain on the edges of mainstream practice and receive minimal exposure.

Here co-operation with those who use the written text is crucial, as discussion of these products can then be brought into all areas of activity within and outside the academic institution. To date relatively little has been written on feminist video practice; access to examples is difficult, availability of viewing infrequent. This increases the importance of making videos within the educational establishment, where a 'ready' audience can be found. Archives of material can be set up for future generations of students and staff. And the establishment of video as a legitimate academic/creative practice will encourage others to participate.

Armes (1988, p. 3) points to the limitations so far of the theoretical analysis of film, arguing that film has not been studied as a social text or interpreted in terms of formal analysis, but the film image has been discussed as metaphor, with, for example, the almost complete exclusion of soundtrack. (Silverman 1988 is an exception.) There is, therefore, room to develop the analysis of video and its interrelation with film in these areas. 'What is required is a conception of a relation within which media technologies are constituted, which is simultaneously individual and collective, internal and external, ... both social and psychic' (Cubitt 1991, p. 16). And further, in extending the discussion of these media, their differing methods of production need to be emphasised.

There are obviously technical particularities to video which affect what we see and hear. Video-tape does not register the same detail and texture that a 16mm film does, for example, but it does have particular visual qualities of its own that can be exploited. The intimate scale of the image affects the viewer's reception of it compared with large-screen projection. The tape can be seen in much more varied circumstances or settings than mainstream film can; by a single individual through to a large group. Editing video is very different from editing film, where the film-stock is physically cut and rejoined. In video, each part has to be synchronised and laid on to the 'master' tape, but the equipment can be used spontaneously as the material is laid down, playing with dissolves, freeze frames, split-screen effects, superimposition, colourisation, tonal variation, the use of other image sources to combine with the videoed material and further layering of sound.

Because sound and image, in the initial recording with the video camera, can be locked into the same tape simultaneously, it encourages 'true to life' recording with long takes. However, in the editing suite extremely artificial effects can be created out of 'documentary' material, so there is a tension between the assumption of video's ability to record 'the real' and its ability to distance from that 'reality' and make the viewer very conscious of the manipulation and construction of the image. 'Video is literal and actual but not necessarily realistic and never real' (Armes 1988, p. 193). An example that helps to illustrate this is a student's video which employed techniques of documentary film using shots of the private and public spaces of Newham, where she worked. These images were collaged with those of graffiti and newspaper headlines to the accompaniment of running commentary by Black and white women about their experiences of racism in that area of London. The soundtrack was very direct and 'real' and enhanced the veracity of the street scenes and interiors, but sometimes the image was manipulated by exaggerating colour contrast or by freezing to create uncomfortable, surreal dissonances, more appropriate to the spoken narratives of the women.

Video production has adopted from film production the detailed film script and pre-planning before a film is embarked on. Yet, in practice, our students have frequently adopted a more 'intuitive' approach to their use of material, trying things out at the editing stage, playing around with effects, going out to record more material halfway through editing, and so on. This is a freedom that video, as opposed to film, offers and perhaps it is a more appropriate use of this medium. Of course it could be argued that this 'hit and miss' approach is a sign of incompetence and not part of professional practice, or that it is a way of working which is particular to these women. But it illustrates that the women felt less constrained by the conventions of the past, by professional rules, and were more willing to open up different modes of production, unscripted and improvised.

Feminist Video Practice

Video-practice as an independent creative activity, as opposed to its commercialised uses as home-movie or TV records or for surveillance, builds on the legacy of women artists from the 1970s who chose alternative media over mainstream painting and sculpture and who were virtually excluded from the production of other mainstream media such as TV and film. They were interested in time-based performance, the interrelation of text and image, as a means to critique established representations and narratives. The world of painting was associated with the touch of the male 'genius', and that of film and text with familiar narrative structures. Video had no history, no specific identity of its own, and so, it was thought, could be used more freely than paint or the written word to question conventions of representation and media production.

Whereas male artists' use of video in the 1970s and 1980s was concerned primarily with the technical, formal aspects of the medium (the work of Nam June Paik is perhaps best known), female video artists' concerns were, and are, principally psychological and focus on personal histories (as does, for example, Catherine Elwes' 'With Child', from 1984). They relate narratives of fantasy and realities; external representations are fused with interiorised experiences expressed by way of sound, speech, overlayed images, sharply cut sequences and transformations of the image in the editing process, such as changes of colour and speed. (An example of this is shown in 'Emergence' by Pratihba Parmar, from 1986.)

Despite a common assumption that we live in a primarily literary culture in Britain, with the consequent undervaluing of visual art in the public realm and in academia, it is the *visual* representations of men and women which are so powerfully manipulated in the public sphere and which inform our everyday experience. Video can be used to address those visual representations directly and reconstruct them, but also to display lives which are neglected or hidden, to make them seen and to allow women who have felt silenced literally to speak their experiences. (This is movingly shown in Jacqui Duckworth's 'Coming Out Twice' from 1991.) One student, for instance, made a video on attitudes to ageing by women in which she allowed the subjects to talk directly to the camera, that is to the viewer; nothing intervened.

Although I know that this is a controversial point, it could be argued that that the medium itself has 'feminine' characteristics which are most appropriate for the telling of women's personal histories and fantasies, and for undermining authoritarian fixities. These 'feminine' signs have been associated with negative definitions of identity but can be transformed into positive characteristics. Video can be seen as fragmentary, complex, delicate (subtle), intimate, emotive, layered; able to break down the clear distinction between self and other, subject and viewer, internal and external. The changing, mobile effects help to suggest shifting identities and meanings and to critique fixed subjectivities. The fleeting narratives, exposed through time, have a relationship to the viewer that is different from that of the written text. The combination of sound and moving image is more emotionally charged, more visceral, than a written text. The impact is immediate and direct and, as I have mentioned earlier, in many ways closer to human experience. Video lends itself to feminist discourse about 'writing with the body', 'speaking from the margins' and 'expressing an alternative language', exhorted for example by Cixous: 'write yourself, your body must make itself heard' (Cixous and Clement 1986, p. 97). (This is manifested in a variety of ways in video, such as Jayne Parker's 'K', from 1990, or Mona Hatoum's 'Measures of Distance', from 1986.) One of our students made a video which was a wordless poem of sound and images conveying the mysterious and contradictory nature of sisterhood, both in terms of her own relationship with her sibling and as metaphor for a wider application. It included passages in which the nude body, clothes, domestic rituals and family photographs were overlayed and interconnected in a rhythmical evocation of a journey.

There is a constant tension between the verbal and the non-verbal. The female voice on the soundtrack can be used to contrast with the expected authoritative, authorial, male voice. Further, she can question her position and relation to the images by the *way* she uses her voice. The female voice is heard and actively present (unlike the written text, where feminist theorists have been accused of writing with a 'male voice'). Silence can also be used in video in a positive and active way as a critique of conventional communication and can contribute a sense of unease and fear to undermine the conventional meanings implied by images. (A good example of this is found in 'Reassemblage' by Trinh Minh-ha, from 1988.)

The use of video can be seen to oscillate between two poles, from that of the documentary to that of the art video. For women, the manipulation of video as documentary is useful to bring alive personal experience, stories of everyday life, and to relate them very directly to viewers and video-maker. It seems to be less distanced from the 'reader' than a written text; the subjects are *present*, speaking with their own voice, and the moving image through time gives a sense of enacting in the present, immediacy, an impression of constant *becoming*, which has in itself a feminist political potential.

Video recordings, then, have the ability to be very direct, unpretentious, to offer traces of everyday events. The camera is relatively light; it can be manipulated in any setting, public or private, by a single individual if need be. The tapes are relatively cheap and can be allowed to run, much as audiotapes can be used to capture conversations. Video's commercial history has encouraged its use as 'home-movie' material, recording leisure activities, but its institutional use, as I have mentioned, has been that of surveillance. Both extremes of private and public use presuppose its accurate and truthful recording of 'reality'.

Feminist video-makers have exploited this characteristic to record 'truthful' everyday, personal experiences in defiance of public constructions of women's lives and stereotypical, generalised images of women. Video-makers such as Jo Spence have played on the 'amateur' use of image, sound and editing to emphasise the intimacy and the particularity of the recordings and that they can be constructed by anyone, are not the exclusive terrain of 'experts'. Her techniques contrast forcefully with the 'professional' products of TV or film production which require a large team of specialists to display technical virtuosity and to present an impersonal, authoritative gloss on the subject.

This feminist documentary approach, moreover, while drawing the viewer into intimate association with the subject, simultaneously makes the viewer acutely aware of how the recording was made. This may be further emphasised by the subject addressing the camera/viewer directly, both to bring them into dialogue but also to make them conscious of their relation to the subject. This consciousness includes the manipulation of the medium; without smooth camera techniques, with conversational voice-over, the viewer is made aware of the intervention of the medium, the way the image is selected, framed, edited and related to the sound or silence, in contrast to the seamlessly constructed narratives in mainstream production in which documentary effects are taken for granted as 'natural'. Further, this self-consciousness of the way realities are constructed through a medium is, I think, made apparent more easily through using video than in written text. One student played with this idea in a video she made which explored the relationship of women and girls to technology. She mixed filmic genres, using 'home-movie' material, her single-handed interviewing of subjects on location and mainstream documentary style, which of course highlighted the production and interpretation of each genre.

The other extreme of the art video allows for a wonderfully rich set of possibilities in the manipulation of images and sounds and can be completely free from narrative conventions. It can blur the boundaries between fact and fiction, fantasy and reality, self and other – which, again, is arguably easier to do in this medium than with written text. (Good examples are 'Faded Wallpaper' by Tina Keane, from 1987, and Susan Hiller's 'Belshazzar's Feast', from 1986.)

The multiplicity of interpretations possible with a video is greater than that of a written text, simply because of the variety of signifying systems at play. The viewer takes a very active part in creating meanings. This can of course cause difficulties for the feminist video-maker who would need to articulate a 'hierarchy' of meanings within the work if she wished a particular feminist viewpoint to dominate the interpretations. Feminist readings would naturally depend on the viewer's knowledge of debates about representation, power relations and critique of mainstream practices. If the video-maker has a preferred reading, she will have to direct the viewer clearly through manipulation of effects and speech and, perhaps, limit the audience. Other feminist video-makers wish to leave interpretations as open as possible, with all the risks of misrepresentation that might entail. There is a tension between attempting to control meanings, which it could be argued is in any case an impossibility, and on the other hand giving a dangerously open (and thus weakened?) presentation. This tension cannot easily be resolved.

Video and the Academy

Visual material, in our culture, is assumed to occupy an area that is non-intellectual, subjective, uncontrolled, open, contingent, natural; in fact to possess those very features that are made to typify in a negative way the common notion of the 'feminine'. These elements disturb the academy because they are seen as outside analysis and assessment. (For a similar reason, personal experience and address have been excluded from written material within the academy.)

Assessment is a form of control which attempts to universalise production and establish a normative value of excellence. Those working in educational establishments will be conscious of the stranglehold that assessment can have over creative, imaginative, provocative work. Assessment procedures and criteria often seem to lead the educational process and product and to constrain the individual, to discourage experimentation and risk. Women's Studies courses are in a cleft stick; on the one hand they must conform to the conventions of the academy in order to be taken seriously, and on the other their pledge is to undermine the academy which has had such a powerful bias in content and methodology and to expose academic 'objectivity' for the sham that it is. Both students and staff are aware of this tension and have difficulty walking the tightrope between.

Because of video's lack of history and the novelty of video production in the academic establishment, video offers greater freedoms and room to experiment; the academy can be taken by surprise. As a terrain of resistance and refusal video can be inserted as a shock within the academic norms. Video-practice allows an open space, not fenced in by the preconceived practices which restrain written work.

Much has been made in recent publications on Women's Studies (such as Richardson and Robinson 1993, p. 49) of the dangers of the domination of feminist theory over practice. The élitism of feminist discourse is seen as remote from women's experiences and from the practical application of feminisms in order to change women's lives. Can video practice help to fill the gap between these two modes of action? It can explore intellectual issues within feminist theories but remain on the margins of academic controls, and it can bring representations of women's thoughts, lives and actions into the sphere of the academy, in a powerful and visible way.

Working within the Institution

One reason we initiated a video dissertation as an alternative to a written dissertation was to allow students the opportunity to use a complex technology for themselves. It has become a cliché that women are not encouraged to use machinery (except in an administrative, secretarial capacity or in the kitchen), and there are relatively few technicians or film-makers who are women.

Because we are so familiar with mainstream cinema and TV our expectation is high that any moving image will be of a conventional narrative structure made with highly complex (but hidden) techniques. One of the early processes for the students is to discover the peculiarities of video as a medium in order to release its creative potential, rather than to attempt to reproduce mainstream film narratives and effects which have been made with enormous budgets and large teams and are shown on a monumental scale. The intimacy and scale of video lend themselves to more private, personal products. For example, one student used the techniques and genres of mainstream cinema, gently mocking them, to relate a complex mythic narrative in which her other self was a talking animated crab and a detective was 'played' by a dressmaker's dummy. The film references were wittily observed, with some footage interspersed with the intimate location of the student's room. It was a private drama about identity and the transformative power of technology.

Although camera use and editing can be controlled by a single individual, it is also possible to work with other students in a co-operative venture. Women's Studies has always promoted collective endeavour as well as personal experience and stressed the links between the two. The staff assumed that the video dissertation would foster group project work, unlike the written dissertation where the assumptions of single authorship are still strong. However, interestingly, during the four years of the course so far each student has elected to work on her own particular project. Group activity has only manifested itself when smaller course tasks are being completed, such as the summer research preparation project (for which students establish familiarity with equipment and test out ideas before launching on their main video dissertation); or as a support group for the individuals working on their videos, helping with source material, venues for filming and advice. Is this due to the hidden pressure of the academic establishment to value individual pieces of work over group work, a pressure which students themselves interiorise? Certainly issues of assessment may come in here. The students may feel worried that their individual contribution will be subsumed in the whole; in a society where individualism is ideologically at the root of our cultural and political structures, it is difficult to attempt to work differently. But more importantly, perhaps, each student becomes passionately involved with the topic she wishes to explore in her video dissertation and the differences between each one's interests, social and political background, and allegiance to different feminisms, means that diversity is inevitable. And it is this diversity of approach and topic which is exciting.

Each student has drawn on her personal life-history or experience in constructing the video, but the personal agenda is rarely explicit in the finished video. Usually this agenda surfaces in the log-book, a space where students can record experiences throughout the year and which can take on a diary-like form (in contrast to the academic contextualising essay they have to submit with the video and log-book). The log-book is a 'private' space and does not have to conform to any format, hence its use for personal explorations. In contrast, in making the video the students are encouraged to consider the audience and so to construct the video for public viewing, however private those circumstances of viewing might be. So far, the students have rejected a directly 'confessional' approach, as found in Jo Spence's 'Video Diary', from 1990, for instance. They have transformed their personal experience into a wider contextual argument that has political potential for others. The work balances delicately between the private and public, and signals the interrelation of these two spheres.

What alternatives to the written dissertation does the video allow? The images are juxtaposed with spoken words or music or other recorded sound, and the images themselves can be layered, adding further richness to interpretation (see earlier sections in this chapter). In playing with techniques, images and sound the students need to signal clearly their consciousness of the feminist debates and methods which they are adopting, as difficulties can arise in assessment. For example, adopting so-called anti-professional or 'amateur' modes as a feminist practice can be interpreted as incompetence which ought to have been overcome in production. So assessment difficulties relate to the undermining of 'normal' expectations of filmic practice and in relation to the work as an 'art' product which does not conform to conventions of documentary narrative. And yet, I think that with video, assessors are more open to new approaches than when students attempt radical changes in the production of their written work. (It is interesting that 'creative work', whether in visual images or written, is that which does not conform to academic practice, which supposes that 'academic' practice is not creative.)

With the help and advice of the students, changes have been made to the expectations of work set up at the start of the course. These are now more flexible. For example, the summer research preparation project had been set up as a compulsory interview exercise, in order for students to learn related skills. However, the students felt it exploited the interviewee, using her as a mere vehicle for their own training, and they made an excellent protest video. Now students choose whatever topic or material they wish to use for this exercise. Students have also made shorter video pieces as part of their first-year essay work, which surprised and delighted staff, and this is now a built-in possibility for the course. Another shift has been away from the prescriptive requirements for assessment, following a film-maker's format to a more open set of video, essay and log-book, which can be used by the student in a variety of ways.

The final videos made by the students display a range of possibilities available to a feminist video-maker. Some have been indicated in examples already cited here. A variety of documentary techniques were used to explore areas of concern close to the student's own experience. At the other extreme, although it is perhaps a mistake to polarise them in this way, art videos have been made using extremely imaginative techniques and juxtapositions of images and sound to open up subjects for discussion, such as a video which combined images of the student's body together with paeleolithic drawing found in caves to develop understanding about the myths and taboos around menstrual and birth blood. Another student used different methods for each video she made. She saw them as a development, starting with a documentary recording of her young daughter and friends talking about their understanding of feminism. There followed a metaphorical piece using images of her friends swimming, 'an alternative to Jacques Lacan'. The third piece was a personal, hermetic evocation set to music reflecting on her identity. The final video stemmed from interviews with Adrian Piper and a close friend and explored the issues of power, marginality and difference, which she saw as a culmination of the themes and methods of the previous works. There is no consistent pattern in the student products. What they all have in common is a feminist agenda in terms of material and treatments and an integration of personal and collective experience.

When I speak of my own experience through my work, I do not attempt to impose my views on another woman. Rather,

I offer my tapes as an invitation to examine her own life and add her perceptions to the collective voice of women's creativity. (Elwes 1990, p. 31.)

Note

1.   I have referred to the video work of students from the Women's Studies MA at Anglia Polytechnic University – Sue Bonnett, Marcene Hayden-Myrie, Mary Knox, Alison Paice, Sue Lewis, Marilyn Jones, Elspeth Owen – and I wish to thank them.

References and Further Reading

Aaron, J. and S. Walby, eds (1991), *Out of the Margins: Women's Studies in the Nineties* (London: Falmer).

Armes, R. (1988), *On Video* (London: Routledge).

Cixous, H. and C. Clement (1986), *The Newly Born Woman* (Minneapolis: University of Minnesota Press).

Cubitt, S. (1991), *Timeshift: On Video Culture* (London: Routledge).

Elwes, C. (1990), *Mothers*, ed. A. Kingston (Birmingham: Ikon Gallery).

Fiske, J. and J. Hartley (1989), *Reading Television* (London: Routledge).

Gray, A. (1992), *Video Playtime: The Gendering of Leisure Technology* (London: Routledge).

Hinds, H., A. Phoenix, and J. Stacey, eds (1992), *Working Out: New Directions for Women's Studies* (London: Falmer).

Iles, C., ed. (1990), *Sign of the Times* (Oxford: Museum of Modern Art).

Kaplan, E.A. (1983), *Women and Film: Both Sides of the Camera* (London: Methuen).

Kennedy, M., C. Lubelska and V. Walsh, eds (1993), *Making Connections: Women's Studies, Women's Movements, Women's Lives* (London: Taylor & Francis).

Kuhn, A. (1982), *Women's Pictures: Feminism and Cinema* (London: Routledge).

Mayne, J. (1990), *The Woman at the Keyhole: Feminism and Women's Cinema* (Indianapolis: Indiana University Press).

Richardson, D. and V. Robinson, eds (1993), *Introducing Women's Studies* (London: Macmillan).

Silverman, K. (1988), *The Acoustic Mirror: The Female Voice in Psychoanalysis and Cinema* (Indianapolis: Indiana University Press).

Turner, G. (1988), *Film as Social Practice* (London: Routledge).

15

Roses and Thorns: Modest Thoughts on Prickly Issues

JOANNA DE GROOT

While it could and certainly should be argued that *all* forms of academic study and scholarship have important personal dimensions for their practitioners, however much this may be minimised or dismissed, those dimensions have clearly been significant for practitioners of Women's Studies. This is regularly recognised and debated by writers, students, and teachers in the field, although often in informal, anecdotal forms expressive of the intimate links which they all sense between personal engagement in intellectual endeavour (learning, writing, teachinq, research) and its structured and public presentation in texts and courses.

Such links are of course part of the history of Women's Studies as a critical intervention in the academy, closely associated with a wider range of social, political, and cultural interventions by and for women which have characterised the last quarter-century or so. As women addressed inequalities in their work and wages, violence and sexual abuse, and blind or biased cultural stereotypes and policy assumptions, so the intellectual work of researching, conceptualising and disseminating information and analyses in such areas developed as a logical adjunct of public debate, cultural activity and social action.

This work was (and is) also a challenge in its own right to the prevalent gender bias and gender blindness of established scholarship, with its misconception, silencing and marginalisation of the female half of humanity as proper and necessary topics for and contributors to social scientific enquiry, historical research and cultural analysis. The general association between Women's Studies and other critical and emancipatory projects undertaken by and for women is paralleled by the personal investment made by those struggling and teaching in the field, and it is the implications of both the general association and the individual investment on which I wish to reflect here.

My reflections are those of someone who began an academic engagement with Women's Studies nearly 20 years ago, and who has been teaching Women's Studies courses at graduate level for ten years, as well as being involved with research in the field. Beyond that, my engagement with Women's Studies has been shaped by my training and practice as a historian, my interest in theory, concept and method, my experiences of political activism, and my work in Middle East Studies. The specific impact of these influences on my outlook will, I hope, become clear as the discussion proceeds, but I have chosen to use notions of 'history' / 'histories' to frame a general approach to my exploration of the 'personal' dimensions of Women's Studies as I have experienced them.

Initially I want to address the issue of the demands and assumptions with which people come to Women's Studies under the heading 'Bringing Histories *to* Women's Studies'. Second, I want to reflect on the content and subject matter of Women's Studies courses through a consideration of 'Learning Histories *in* Women's Studies'. Lastly, I will suggest that the experiences of each cohort of students working in Women's Studies for a specific period, and of groups of teachers accumulating practice in the field over the years, both contribute to 'Making Histories *of* Women's Studies'.

My reasons for choosing this approach are twofold: first, history as a discipline is partly constituted around the problematic of relationships between *persons* and circumstances, and is deeply imbued with a concern for the 'voice of the past' – that is, 'personal' subject matter – and as such has shaped my own cultural formation; second, the notion of 'history' allows me to do justice to the roles of *process* and of *time* as they have affected both myself and others who have shared with me the experience of 'doing' Women's Studies.

Bringing Histories *to* Women's Studies

From the time of first planning a syllabus and interviewing applicants for the MA in Women's Studies with which I have been involved for a decade, the issue of personal investments has loomed large. This has not just been a matter of the enthusiasm of students and staff for the project, or the continuing need to explain and defend it within an uninformed, suspicious, sometimes hostile community, although both these factors feature significantly in the everyday experience of those involved in the course. The commitment which fuels both advocacy and enthusiasm for Women's Studies is sustained by a whole range of specific personal expectations, assumptions and demands. Staff and students look to Women's Studies *to meet important needs* which they have evolved quite independently of the subject or the courses. This generates very powerful tensions between their hopes and ideals and the actualities of a real course undertaken under real constraints (personal, institutional, material, intellectual). The source of these needs lies within the personal histories of individual students and staff, but is legitimised by the historic and structural relationships between Women's Studies and a whole spectrum of women's aspirations. The energies, frustrations and challenges arising from the encounter between needs and desires generated by past experience and the present realities of a Women's Studies course, and the subsequent transformation of both, merit fuller discussion.

The past experiences which shape women's demands on Women's Studies may be specifically academic and intellectual, or they may be part of the broader field of hopes and dissatisfaction in their lives. These may be generated by personal encounters with male violence or discrimination at work, by working with or for women on a community project or artistic endeavour, or by the desire to change relationships with partners, colleagues or children. Experiences of studying or teaching academic subjects where opportunities to consider women are denied or denigrated are an obvious and frequent source of powerful determination to recover and reconstruct teaching and learning in women-inclusive ways. Such experiences may also encourage a culture of complaint and conspiracy theory which can positively stimulate creative critical reassessments of much established scholarship, yet may equally well produce a comfortable but unhelpful victim paranoia in which everyone just reassures one another that women get a hard deal in the academy. The real challenge for Women's Studies courses, in my experience, is to foster the critical curiosity produced by participants' awareness of the scholarly marginalisation of women by encouraging a self-reflective approach which *uses* anger constructively to generate rigorous analysis of that phenomenon rather than just repeatedly restating it.

The other broader histories which people bring to Women's Studies often embody the diversities and contradictions contained within/under the 'suitcase' or 'umbrella' term 'women'. Those women primarily conscious of their ethnic, national, class or racial identity, or of their sexuality, age and particular marital or familial experience, may well make that the basis for demanding priority for a particular articulation of female activities, identities, relationships and oppressions. Seminar discussions which encompass forceful challenges from non-English or non-white experience, from lesbian cultures and politics, from the less socially privileged to the more privileged, or from older women with histories of family responsibility to the young, single and childless, provide both threats and opportunities on Women's Studies courses. The most obvious threats are that some or all participants will retreat into wrapping themselves in whatever banner of identity they have chosen, or will refuse to pursue issues for fear either of fracturing fragile group relations or of being seen as less than politically correct. If opportunities to *explore* diversities and *open up* discussion of the various locations and constituents of women's experiences, difficulties, interests and identities are to be realised, all those involved need to be active in seeking alternatives to retreat and refusal. This may include strategies ranging from trust-building exercises at an early stage of the course to regular informal small group meetings to run parallel with formal seminar work, as well as careful facilitation of the seminars themselves. The challenge of providing space and validation for divergent and contentious alternatives without being patronising or protecting them from searching enquiry is one of the major dynamics of teaching and learning in Women's Studies.

What the 'bringing of histories' to Women's Studies foregrounds is the continuing interaction between academic involvement in Women's Studies courses and other aspects of the lives and selves of the staff and students who undertake them. Individual expectations of Women's Studies can be as much about personal agendas (can it help me decide to leave a partner? transform my professional life? compensate for previous disappointments and disadvantages? find/change my political outlook?) as about intellectual needs. However much one knows or is told that academic work can make at best a partial contribution to meeting such wide and complex aspirations, one can still be angry and disappointed when expectations are not met. That anger and disappointment are easily projected on to fellow students and staff and can be interwoven destructively rather than creatively with teaching and learning. It seems to me that such legitimate responses do need to be expressed, but that this should be done within appropriate boundaries, and with mutual recognition of both the wish to seek positive outcomes (rather than just engaging in blaming) and the fact that there will be limits to what is possible. Having said that, I have found it heartening and affirmative to share the painful but productive negotiations which can and do emerge when participants deal with their feelings and with each other in a constructive way, whether through considered critiques and transformations of the course, or through nurturing closer, more thoughtful, relationships among themselves.

Learning Histories *in* Women's Studies

If diverse and changing female histories and expectations are characteristic of what students and staff bring to Women's Studies, they are equally part of the agenda for teaching and learning which is on offer once they are involved. For most of us it is a matter of expanding and disaggregating the category 'women', through exploring the diverse situations, activities, experiences and relationships which shape/have shaped and are/have been shaped by women, and by enhancing whatever disciplinary perspectives and skills we have acquired with others. While there are real debates and difficulties around the use of inter/cross/trans-disciplinary approaches to the study of women, the benefits of confronting or combining, say, cultural and textual analysis with investigative and analytical study of social phenomena or with historical perspectives are significant. This has been evident in situations ranging from a seminar discussion which situates Charlotte Perkins Gilman's text *The Yellow Wallpaper* not only within American feminist thought and writing but also within histories of medicine and race relations in the US, to a student's research on women's political lives in Italy between the 1930s and 1950s using oral history, archives, literary theories of narrative and philosophical debates on 'the self'. Such processes can be challenging and uncomfortable, as people's existing assumptions about how to examine and explain women's lives come under question. Ideas that one situation is typical of all ('religion always oppresses women') or that one category of explanation or material is more relevant or powerful than another ('novels can't tell you about the real world') can be quite hard to give up, especially if they seem to be validated by someone's own history and experience.

It is therefore crucial for Women's Studies to provide opportunities to expand, disaggregate and test our concepts and knowledge about women, to *go beyond* the existing knowledge and experience of participants. Exposure to a range of disciplinary skills and frameworks enriches the resources available to scholars and students, clarifying their appreciation of both the valuable specificities of particular disciplines and the possible relationships and interactions between them. Women need to set their own histories alongside the histories of others in a comparative, critical, pluralistic fashion in which full acknowledgement of diversities in time, space and social location is the prerequisite for any useful synthesising, conceptual or explanatory work. The process of accumulating and assessing material which expresses such diversities provides the immediate satisfaction of increasing knowledge and curiosity, and the challenge of attempting to value and account for the histories of others. Commitment to pluralism and diversity is not a matter of following fashionable trends, but rather an expression and condition of the intellectual vitality and relevance of Women's Studies.

This commitment has the effect not only of opening up the category 'women' to richer, more vigorous discussion and investigation, but also of drawing attention to the complex, even problematic, relationship between 'experience' and 'knowledge' in Women's Studies. Much of the power and energy in women's self-activity (whether social, intellectual or political) has come from their capacity and determination to describe and use their own experiences, challenging the ways in which these have been marginalised, misrepresented or devalued. However, unreflective emphasis on and acceptance of the category of 'experience', and celebration of 'finding a voice/making visible', are problematic for Women's Studies. Certainly these processes can all too easily confine practitioners at the level of assertion and description, rather than encouraging us to be active in seeking meaning and making sense of our (diverse) experiences. Perhaps the first step in moving from the former to the latter is the recognition that the very act of speaking about lives and experiences gives these a cultural and discursive construction, and offers interpretation as well as information. A woman speaking of physical pain to a doctor, a political activist describing experiences of work with other women in a mixed organisation, a group of mothers exchanging views about the care of children, operate with notions of 'health', 'politics' or 'mothering' which they have acquired, modified and used within their particular historical and social settings. These notions have been developed within such settings both by individual women and by those operating the familial, communal, religious and educational systems within which people learn, develop and are socialised. They are the products of historic contestations and negotiations over meaning (Is PMT an 'illness'? What is the 'proper' way to raise children? Is taking minutes at party meetings 'political'?) which create the means whereby we 'know' life/ourselves/the world and express that 'knowledge'. When women speak about their lives/experiences/situations, they select and construct their accounts within this framework which creates an intimate relationship between existence and discourse.

It can be argued that it is more appropriate to accept and explore such close links rather than to create a misleading analytical separation between what in reality are interdependent aspects of people's lives. Instead of being characterised as 'raw data', people's accounts of their lives are better understood, and valued, as culturally embedded and conceptually developed. A critical view might hold that claims to 'authenticity' or 'uniqueness' in a particular person's narrative or description are undercut by an approach that draws attention to the shaping role of cultural meanings and the integral relationship between discursive, cultural elements and other dimensions of human experience. However, since the cultural, discursive construction or expression of experience is also a human activity, those engaged in that activity are not just the prisoners of convention, but are engaged in accepting, changing or subverting the cultural practices they acquire. Whether assessing women's fiction, analysing women's past testimony (oral or written) or using contemporary interview material, Women's Studies work which acknowledges this approach will indeed allow women full respect and intellectual/cultural agency. Rather than patronisingly dealing with what women say as mere 'evidence', researcher and researched meet on the same terrain as human beings dealing with experience. Thus the initially painful process of treating one's own experience as relative, or of exposing valuable material provided by women to critical assessment rather than unquestioning endorsement, can become a creative exploration, reintegrating the categories life/experience and understanding/analysis at another level.

What emerges from this discussion, which obviously does not exhaust consideration of how experience is processed in Women's Studies, is that there is indeed a *learning* process involved as the agendas brought in by particular staff and students encounter others. There are real personal and intellectual difficulties involved in discovering that one's own history/experience/perspective may well be challenged rather than confirmed, and those difficulties merit recognition and attention. Nonetheless, it does nobody any service to avoid them, and thereby remain in a closed and unreflective space, denying the opportunity for active engagement in comparison, commentary and critique which will ultimately increase comprehension and confidence instead of (as many fear) undermining them. Where Women's Studies moves people past such fears and supports them in the processes of thinking and learning about women by addressing the issues raised here, it can meet personal and intellectual needs which are real and important.

Making Histories *of* Women's Studies

The frequent use of the term 'process' that has characterised my reflections is a reminder that 'doing' Women's Studies is an activity which is itself undertaken over a period of time, and therefore has a 'history' for each participant. I need only consider the ten cohorts of MA students who have worked with me and my colleagues to become vividly aware both of how each cohort has changed and created its own history over its own one or two years of work, and how cumulatively students and staff have shaped a longer history over the whole decade. Again, it is useful to see these histories which have been made as comprising the lived/described experiences of participants, and also as a cultural evolution and intellectual development to which they have contributed.

The personal dimension of making histories in Women's Studies is the product of encounters and interactions between individuals who frequently find themselves in contradictory relationships with one another. Common commitment to the subject and the course exists in tension with the necessarily diverse views, histories, expectations and approaches within a large group. Such tension does not simply remain unchanged for any particular cohort, but rather creates a dynamic which sometimes isolates individuals or fractures the cohort into distinct, even antagonistic groups (for example, politicos and intellectuals, lesbians and heteros, older and younger students), and can equally create empathies and solidarities. All these shift over time and feed into the intellectual work being undertaken in ways which produce both exciting and demanding situations in seminars. How people prove a scholarly issue, what restraints, challenges or enthusiasms they express, is in part a function of the personal dynamics among a group of staff and students and the tensions, bonds or divisions they have created among themselves. An argument over Simone de Beauvoir may well embody the inequalities in educational privilege which differentiate the participants as much as disagreements about her ideas. Interest in a particular text or theory may be the badge of membership of some clique as well as a response to ideas and material.

Staff members of the group often feel the pressure to monitor and take responsibility for group dynamics in order to protect, encourage or facilitate useful outcomes in difficult situations. Students feel the demands both of their relationships with peers and with the teachers and structures of the course. Fears about academic study, difficulties with the relationships between 'study', 'life' and 'politics', and challenges arising from the learning processes discussed earlier, fuse with particular pleasures and enthusiasms in evolving distinctive combinations in each cohort. Such combinations are expressed in painful confrontations and rejections, in energetic, creative work to resolve problems or differences, and in many gestures of support and solidarity. Individual experience and group identity(ies) feed into and out of the work and the human dynamics of the course, and come to constitute a significant part of what people remember and historicise as what Women's Studies means/has meant for them as teachers, learners and scholars.

However, that legacy of history and memory is not just the individual inheritance of each person involved in Women's Studies; it is also a collective inheritance which is created and used by groups. The lives and work of former students are energised by their reflections on the history of their involvement, just as similar reflections provide a point of departure for the reassessment and development of Women's Studies courses by teaching staff. The sense of identity and opportunities for creative work provided by Women's Studies, and the difficulties and criticisms it generates, are both a historic personal asset for each individual involved and the shared resource of collective history. There is of course tension between the individual histories and memories and joint or common elements which are shared by some or all participants. However, the point to make is that reflection, assessment and comparison of experiences and histories created by varied individuals in different years, courses and institutions is more than a random collection of personal histories. We can comment on, learn from and disseminate views of 'doing Women's Studies' in ways which inform colleagues and successors, establishing narratives and traditions for them to use. In this sense histories of Women's Studies are a rich and challenging resource from our past which can shape learning, teaching and scholarship in the present and future.

By Way of Conclusion

My own personal history of engagement with Women's Studies encompasses all the elements on which I have reflected here. It is difficult to draw up any balance between the difficulties, hurts and constraints I have encountered in teaching, learning and making history within Women's Studies, and the pleasures, creative changes and rewards I have obtained. Probably the notion of balancing is not especially useful, and I am better off simply acknowledging and valuing the full range of anxiety, excitement, anger and sadness which I have experienced. Roses do have thorns. I also recognise that my 'history' is interwoven with and shaped by, as well as shaping, the other histories made by colleagues, students and scholars within Women's Studies. Above all, however, I would want to argue that it is the slippery, complex but real interconnection of personal histories and scholarly and intellectual activity, rather than the distinction between them, which is integral to what Women's Studies has been, is and will be.

Index